NHS Trusts in Practice

Edited by

Edward Peck & Peter Spurgeon

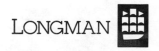

Longman Group UK Limited
Westgate House, The High, Harlow, Essex CM20 1YR
Telephone (0279) 442601
Fax (0279) 444501

First published 1993   *1066146 8*

A catalogue record for this book is available from the British
Library.

ISBN 0–582–22860–3

Printed in Great Britain by BPCC Wheatons Ltd, Exeter

Contents

Contents vii

Contributors

Edward Peck   Centre for Mental Health Services Development,
Kings College London

Peter Spurgeon   Health Services Management Centre,
University of Birmingham

Cliff Graham   Institute of Health
Kings College London

Lynn Ashburner   Centre for Corporate Strategy and Change,
University of Warwick

John Dennis   Chief Executive
Richmond, Twickenham and Roehampton Healthcare NHS Trust

Chris West   Chief Executive
Portsmouth and South East Hampshire Health Commission

Judy Hargadon   Chief Executive
Croydon Community NHS Trust

Mike Fry   Chief Executive
Christie Hospital NHS Trust

Eric Caines   Director
Centre for Health Services Management,
University of Nottingham

Andrew Wall   Health Services Management Centre,
University of Birmingham

1 Introduction

Edward Peck and Peter Spurgeon

The proposal to create 'Self Governing Hospitals' contained in 'Working for Patients' (1989) generated a political, professional and public debate on the NHS, the like of which had probably not been seen since the 1940s. The performance of NHS trusts has become the bench mark against which the Conservative Government has been attempting to demonstrate the success of the package of reforms heralded in 'Working for Patients'. The messages emanating from the government, the Department of Health and National Health Services Management Executive have, therefore, been uniformly up-beat and optimistic. Many NHS managers were similarly positive about the greater freedoms and autonomy they saw as associated with Trust status. Obviously this was especially true of those managers who sought Trust status in the first and second waves.

Much of the criticism of trusts has been just as partisan and often appears to be based on a wish to exploit the perceived public suspicion of this innovation. The focus of this concern, strongly fuelled by rather sensational media coverage, was whether trusts somehow sat just outside the old NHS, and represented the first stage of an agenda for an enlarged private provision. The degree and emotion attached to the reforms has led to limited opportunity for dispassionate and impartial evaluation.

Of course hard data acceptable to all interested parties is difficult to identify. Nonetheless a great deal of experience has been formed and this book represents an opportunity to research and assess progress in terms of original expectations. These chapters, completed around the time that first wave trusts were celebrating their second anniversary, explores perspectives of NHS trusts as the title suggests, in practice. They attempt to understand the experience of NHS trusts in the contexts of the claims made in 'Working for Patients' from a variety of perspectives:

- policy analysts;
- management researchers; and

- managers themselves involved at national, purchaser and provider level.

As a context to these specific contributions, Cliff Graham's chapter places trusts in a historical perspective that takes as its starting point the foundation of the first self governing hospital, Barts, in 1123.

Edward Peck, in his two chapters, reports his research on the formation and performance of a first wave NHS trust board. In an account of a complimentary piece of research, Lyn Ashburner presents her findings from a national survey on the membership of first wave trust boards and the extent to which these findings fulfil the aspirations of the Department of Health and the National Health Services Management Executive. Clearly the nature and role of the new cadre of Non-Executive Directors will prove a major factor in the longer term success of the Trust process.

In Chapter 7, Mike Fry and Judy Hargadon share their personal experiences of guiding a provider unit to first wave trust status and the impact on the organisation and themselves of being a Trust. They also both suggest the further steps that are necessary to release the full potential that they believe Trust status can bring. The purchaser perspective is provided in Chapter 6 by John Dennis and Chris West, the former having returned very recently to a provider role as chief executive of a Trust.

These personal reflections by purchasers and providers are followed appropriately by Peter Spurgeon in Chapter 8 with a discussion of the different stances taken on how the purchaser/provider relationship might operate. Eric Caines has been a strong advocate of trusts and the potential freedoms afforded in terms of new payment systems. He presents his personal view of how the advent of trusts has affected management generally in the NHS.

In contrast Andrew Wall provides an incisive critique of the assumptions and language surrounding the creation of NHS trusts. His chapter examines of these issues from the standpoint of an alternative paradigm of the management of the NHS.

This book does not aspire to a consistent theme, preferring instead to allow readers to make their own judgements about the quality of the arguments presented. Nor does it make any apologies for the mix of styles, moving from personal accounts to academic research. Too often, books present a limited audience with a limited perspective. This book attempts to provide a broad readership with material that addresses the topic from a range of perspectives and approaches.

Although the editors allow themselves the indulgence of a short conclusion to highlight some of the major themes, there is no attempt to produce a neat ending. The intention is to give readers the opportunity to reflect on the experience of NHS trusts in practice in order to explore and challenge their own perspectives. In that sense, this book is an atlas that attempts to plot the terrain rather than a guidebook to help readers to traverse it. Given the number of disparate starting points of the people who will approach this book, then the latter task, would, in any case, have been impossible. It is important to recognise, however, that the creation of Trusts was a means to an end and not an end in itself. As a first wave Trust chairman told the Health Committee, "if one is to achieve an effective split to the purchaser and provider roles . . . you need to do something which clearly introduces some degree of autonomy for the provider . . . the solution, therefore, seems to me is inevitable; some form of structure like a Trust" (Health Committee, 1992). Trusts were a device which would enable Health Authorities to shed management responsibilities and focus on health needs assessment, the development of specifications and the negotiation of contracts within the 'internal market.' Our hope is that the diversity of background of both authors and readers will allow for a self-selecting reassurance of similar views but equally insight into alternative perspectives.

References

HMSO (1989) 'Working for Patients', Cmnd 555, London: HMSO.

2 NHS Trusts: continuity or discontinuity?

Cliff Graham

In the beginning

The first hospital in England opened its doors to the sick and needy poor in 1123 A.D. At that time Saint Bartholomew's Hospital in the prestigious City of London felt it had to stretch out its hand to the poor, unfortunate residents of Hackney and other less well-endowed parts of the capital. Such an institution would not be lacking in 'trust'; it clearly would have 'status'; and, almost by definition, it would be 'self governing'. It is also worth noting that it would be free of national government, prescriptive legislation, and a medical and dental school, or even a university. This might suggest that the concept of self governing trust status can only exist when government, law and the professions are kept out.

At base, therefore, present organisation and management of health services rests upon the 1,000 year old concept of service to the community by the community. It is most important to examine this concept more closely before reaching conclusions about what is needed of health service organisation and management in the 21st Century. In short, what happened in the years between the opening of Barts, and the arrival of its, and the first, medical school in 1762 and, is it significant that the University of London was not founded until almost another century later?

Since these issues are increasingly being looked at in a European and wider international context, it is also important to examine parallel developments at that time in other parts of the world where Britain was such a strong colonial and trading power. For example why did Benjamin Franklin take the concept of the London Hospital in Whitechapel to America, and have it accepted in 1751 as the model for America's first hospital – the Pennsylvania Hospital in Philadelphia – to be founded in that year and opened in 1752, and yet, since then, the USA has rigidly opposed the transfer to the New World of any of the later concepts of health care organisation and management developed in the Mother Country? Why do we lack a common transatlantic approach to the organisation and management of health services?

Similarly, why has the organsation and management of health services in Europe not been more influenced by, or influenced, these developments in the United Kingdom. For example, why is the UK the only country in the European Community with an NHS funded through general taxation and free at the point of service. Was this what Lloyd-George intended when he sent observers to examine the Bismarck insurance system in Germany as part of his preparation for his 1911 National Insurance system?

The Barts beginning suggests, therefore, that a closer examination of the underlying culture and history of health care organisation and management in the United Kingdom should be a prerequisite to any present day consideration of these matters; concentrating in particular on, what appear to be, the more durable conceptions over this period of 'Trust', 'Status' and 'Self Governing'.

The impact of medical education

This cultural and historical perspective would need to be informed also by the key issues related to the development of the main professions in the UK. These developments began to take root about halfway between the foundation of Barts and the beginnings of effective social legislation in the mid 19th Century. The major medical schools began to appear, mainly in London but also in other large cities, over 500 years after the foundation of Barts. But it is surprising to find that the medical schools, and medical education generally, paid little or no attention to the organisation and management of health services, beyond the extension of the 'apprentice' system operating at Barts and the other pre-medical school hospitals under which the junior doctor followed the consultant on the wards until such time as he was judged capable of taking full responsibility for patients and had, therefore, 'completed his apprenticeship'. Indeed, it is possible to assert that there exists no major issue of health policy or organisation and management which has been influenced fundamentally by the policy of medical education; and, that there exists no major aspect of health policy or organisation which has had a fundamental impact on the policy and practice of medical education.

This assessment is not just an academic point, nor is it simply a piece of history. The practical effect of this situation is that we have too many teaching hospitals and medical schools in London, and the other major cities in England; we have too many doctors trained in hospital work, particularly in acute medicine; we have too few community health services, including GP services, in the inner cities; we have no doctors in the 'cinderella' specialties who have been trained to work fully in the community; and, right up until quite recently, we have almost no doctors engaged full time in the organisation and management of health services.

The creation of the Board

The organisation and management of the London teaching hospitals at the time of the foundation of the major medical schools in the 18th Century comprised: a local Board, local leaders in the world of business, banking and the professions, to govern the hospital, serviced by a 'clerk' or 'house governor' not uncommonly drawn from the non-medical professions. Senior doctors, and later matrons, would be represented on the Board. It was all based on the concept of resident, local management and colonial government, military-style organisation. Indeed, the underlying management of the medical work of the hospital reinforced, and maybe gave birth to, this traditional form of organisation, given that the medical consultants in the hospital trained their junior doctors on the 'apprentice' principle. The junior doctor was trained on the job, by walking the wards behind his consultant and watching and doing what he did; a veritable 'pupil master' arrangement which had governed the legal profession since the time of 'Good Queen Bess' and her Inns of Court. On this example, the house governor can be seen as the barristers' clerk who both 'controls' and is 'controlled' by his betters!

It is possible to assert therefore that the medical profession was the first profession to bring about the concept of organisation and management of health services on the basis of 'self governing' institutions of 'status' which earned the 'Trust' of all concerned. The same profession was the first to introduce 'Schools' to control entry to the profession *and* to dictate what should go on inside the institution. This was the beginning of the organisation of the work of the hospital on the basis of the consultant 'firm', which then dictated and directed the use of everyone else's resources without having to manage directly many of these resources themselves. Paradoxically, it is the medical profession which in recent decades has shown itself to be the most ill equipped and disinclined to engage in management matters; and, to be most hostile to any strengthening and expansion of the general management process.

Moving into the 19th Century

By the end of the 19th Century, London University had not only gained the right to extend beyond its founding brief of 1826, to act as a sort of central government department for, *inter alia*, the medical schools but it had also moved into a position of influence and control over the product of medical higher education. This also heralded the new and growing area of health care bureaucracy, in which duplication and triplication of function could be observed, not only in London but also in the other major cities. This also marked the point at which health policy, organisation and management were separated from medical education, manpower and career progression; with the medical schools, universities and professions concentrating on essentially professional matters, leaving organisation and management to government. A century later, these basic divisions of function persist, with occasional outbursts of 'trench warfare' when either side feels its interests are under threat.

On the other hand, public health issues had begun to surface; wars had begun, and would continue, to devastate the institutions and the local communities; the cost of health care began to present problems; and the dominance of the medical profession was beginning to come under challenge. All this provided the ideal setting for the rise of the politician and the bureaucrat. Thus began a century of social legislation stretching from the sewers of the cities through the local government of public health to the socialisation of medicine to the 'Health of the Nation' and the 'Internal Market' for health services.

Disraeli and Chamberlain make an unlikely pairing, in many important respects, but they formed a very powerful conservative duo, in setting the course of public health and local government for the 19th and 20th Centuries. It has taken their many successors, in all political parties, until 1992, over a century after Disraeli, to focus attention on the management and betterment of the 'Health of the Nation', rather than the medical treatment of illness, and to develop the concept of 'Community Care' as a major responsibility of local government rather than the NHS. It has taken a thousand years to reach the present point where we can all recognise and accept that health is more important than illness and that health is the responsibility of every citizen and involves action by every part of government, national and local, in partnership with the private and voluntary sectors and the individual citizen. By the same token, the management and organisation of health care is now seen as the province of general management and not simply or solely, or in many cases even at all of doctors.

It is also a strange fact to report that the sterling work of Disraeli, in producing such all important public services as water and sewage treatment, and Chamberlain, in getting clear the local government arrangements and responsibilities, is now once again under close scrutiny both in terms of the need to renew this infrastructure of public health but also to reform local government and give back to it responsibility for the organisation and management of community care and key aspects of the 'Health of the Nation'. This was the challenge also at the turn of the last century, as it will be at the very beginning of the next millenium.

The 20th Century

The present century of health services organisation and management is dominated by Welsh Giants – Lloyd-George and Aneurin Bevan – and their supporting actors, Beveridge and Churchill (who wrote the first White Paper on a National Health Service in 1944). It also involves other names of influence, perhaps less well known – such as Porritt, who proposed the merger of GPs and hospital and community services; Guillebaud, who pointed out real problems about the cost of the NHS; Robinson, the minister who grasped both these nettles before being swept aside politically by Crossman, who then achieved less; Joseph and Castle who both failed to reorganise the service effectively or usefully; Owen who grasped effectively the findings of the infamous 'Resource Allocation Working Party'; Fowler and Clarke who drove through general management and introduced the beginnings of an internal market at the behest of Thatcher; Griffiths who made general management and community care problems which Government could not ignore; Waldegrave who produced the 'Health of the Nation'; and, finally, Bottomley, who has opened the London and Community Care cans of worms before she has secured her political position, and who takes us back to the beginning with her wish to close Barts after 1,000 years of service.

The century can be divided into two main parts so far: the first 60 years, in which major illnesses and diseases were conquered and the greatest piece of social legislation this century was put in place: the *NHS Act 1946* (the core of which, Section 1, still forms the basis of the Secretary of State's responsibility in the NHS and *Community Care Act 1990*); and, the last 30 years, in which there has been an almost total concentration on issues of organisation and management. This is shown most graphically in the contents of the annual reports of the Department of Health, the Chief Medical Officer, the Medical Officers of Health and the Committees of Parliament. The challenge facing those charged with responsiblity for these important matters in the last half of the last decade of the present century is to develop the underlying issues of health policy and practice required for the 21st Century without losing sight of the meaning of this vast historical perspective and yet make the maximum use of the new tools of organisation and management which have been fashioned through hard work over the past 30 years in particular.

This process can best be assisted by a close examination of the 20 key points in the organisation and management of health services from the establishment of the NHS to date, as follows:

1. The Internal Administration of Hospitals (Central Health Services Council Report) 1954: the only report about managing *inside* the institution, which proposed a single chief officer.

2. The Cost of the National Health Service 1956 'Guillebaud Report': the then Chairman of British Rail reported, inter alia, that '. . . at no level from the Ministry to the hospital is there sufficient consciousness of responsibility for capital assets at all comparable with that felt in a business concern . . .'.

3. Royal Colleges and BMA Medical Services Review Committee 1962 'Porritt Report': this proposed the integration of the Family Practitioner Committees, the Hospital Services and the Community Health Services.

4. The Hospital Plan 1962 under which Enoch Powell, then Minister of Health, proposed to build a whole network of District General Hospitals (an institution more clearly defined in the 1969 'Bonham-Carter Report') and refurbish a good number of existing general hospitals so that all the rest could be closed.

5. The Hospital Building Programme 1966 under which Kenneth Robinson, then Minister of Health, proposed a building programme which could be afforded (it had been estimated that the 'Powell' plan would have required annual capital expenditure of £1bn per annum until the end of the century when the age of the average hospital bed would only have been reduced from 70 years to 50 years and 1960s buildings would then need replacing).

6. The NHS–Administration of Hospital Authorities (Health Circular (68)28) 1968: which drew on the Farquharson-Lang Report in Scotland and required a clear separation between the functions of members of health authorities and the management responsibilities of their chief officers.

7. The Administrative Structure of the Medical and Related Services in England and Wales (first 'Robinson' Green Paper) 1968: which proposed a comprehensive health service, covering hospitals, GPs and local authority services, under the administration of 40 to 50 area boards working direct to the Minister of Health.

8. The Future Structure of the NHS (second 'Crossman' Green Paper) 1970: which proposed the organisation of a unified service based primarily on the various functions which comprise the service – medical, professional and institutional support services – under the administration of about 90 area health authorities with 200 district committees with co-opted members of the local community and NHS staff, and a regional tier with functions carried out by regional offices of the DHSS and existing RHB functions undertaken by regional health councils on which each AHA would be represented.

9. The National Health Service Reorganisation: England ('Joseph' White Paper) 1972, 'which leaned towards management where

the 1970 Green Paper had leaned towards participation', according to its author. It set up high powered 'Working Parties on Collaboration' between the NHS and Local Government and a top level NHS Reorganisation Steering Group and Working Party assisted by management consultants McKinsey & Co (led by the present Secretary of the King's Fund) to devise a structure based on a reorganised DHSS (to be split between 'policy' and 'management' functions) and an NHS comprising 14 RHAs and 90 AHAs; plus about 200 community health councils to match each administrative unit within the AHAs (to which most of the pre-existing members of the Hospital Management Committees and Hospital House Committees were transferred).

10. The NHS Reorganisation Act 1973: which implemented the outcome of the 1972 White Paper deliberations and, crucially, implemented in addition two further proposals without which the then Chief Medical Officer, Sir Goerge Godber, might well have withheld his support for the changes. These changes were: the strengthening and full recognition of the District Management Team (with three doctors in membership – District Community Physician, General Practitioner and Hospital Specialist – out of a total of only six members) as the 'dynamic crucible' through which all the changes would be made effective; and, the implementation of the, ultimately, three 'Cogwheel' reports of the Joint Working Party on the 'Organisation of Medical Work in Hospitals' – the first two of which were completed under his Chairmanship in 1967 (reprinted by him in 1972) and 1972 and the last by his successor, Sir Henry Yellowlees, in 1974.

11. The 'Democracy in the NHS: Membership of Health Authorities' ('Castle' Green Paper) 1974: which proposed to extend the role and influence of CHCs and to increase the number of local authority members on AHAs.

12. The 'Priorities for Health and Personal Social Services in England' ('Castle' Green Paper, 'The Consultative Document') 1976: which set out the options for prioritising services, and therefore limited resources, in the NHS and local government Social Services for the first time ever; and, in particular, led to White Papers on 'Better Services' for the 'Cinderella Specialties' of mental illness, mental handicap, the elderly and children.

13. The 'Sharing Resources for Health in England: Final Report of the Resource Allocation Working Party' (RAWP Report: 'Owen' White Paper) 1976: which, for the first time ever, linked the allocation of resources to the population health need through epidemiological and social profiles. Allocation was to be based on an assessment of health status rather than historical calculations related to the presence of health services.

14. The 'Prevention and Health: Everybody's Business' ('Owen' Green Paper) 1976: which was the forerunner to the 1992 White Paper on 'The Health of the Nation' and for the first time concentrated on health status, which was mainly the result of factors outside the responsibility and scope of the NHS, rather than health services provided by the NHS essentially to cope with ill health and disease.

15. The 'Way Forward' ('Ennals' Green Paper) 1977: which brought into balance the planned intentions of health authorities, resulting from the 1976 NHS Planning System pioneered by David Owen, the national priorities resulting from action on Barbara Castle's consultative document and the resources made available through the Exchequer and distributed according to the RAWP formula (which was sustained through different administrations for over a decade).

16. The 'Royal Commission on the National Health Service' ('Wilson' report designed to take the heat out of doctors' disputes of 1976 about pay and conditions, other union disputes and such issues as agency nurses) 1979: which reported to a Conservative Secretary of State for Social Services – then Mr Patrick – now Lord Jenkin. The eight volume report moved across the shiny desks of the politician and civil servant from the printer to the archivist within a matter of days and weeks, pausing on its journey only to present the politician with a recommendation to abolish the AHAs and not to worry about the growth of the private sector.

17. The 'Patients First' ('Jenkin' Green Paper) 1979: which abolished the AHAs, delegated more responsibility to district services at hospital and unit level, introduced DHAs and simplified the professional advisory machinery and planning system but sustained the concept of 'consensus management'.

18. The 'NHS Management Inquiry' ('Griffiths Report') 1983: which introduced the function of 'General Management' at the expense of the pre-existing 'consensus management', management budgeting, consumer choice and voice, outcome measurement, economic appraisal and, most important, to focus attention on the central importance of management in achieving an effective health service.

19. The 'Community Care: Agenda for Action' ('Second Griffiths Report') 1988: which proposed to hand over responsibility for 'social care' in the community to local government rather than the NHS and to allow local government a say in the assessment of 'medical care', which remained the responsibility of the NHS, whenever this involved community care. This brought together funding from the NHS, local government social services and

housing and education and employment, social security and the private and voluntary sectors.

20. The 'NHS and Community Care Act 1990': which implemented the Government White Paper on 'Working for Patients' and the 'Second Griffiths Report' (where implementation was postponed until April 1993), which introduced the 'internal market' in health, 'self governing' and other 'Trust' units all carrying trust 'Status', separated the 'purchase' (by DHAs and FHSAs) from 'provision' of health services (by 'provider units and hospitals' and 'Fundholding' and other GPs) and strengthened the choice and voice of the consumer by providing that 'money follows the patient' and laying down rights in a 'Patients' Charter'.

The point of all this history, particularly over the last 30 years of this century, is to demonstrate how the NHS has moved inexorably towards the right territory – health status not health services; that it may have done so at the wrong time, when it cannot afford, financially or politically, to do the job properly; that, even so, it may still lack the tools – management skill and organisational arrangement – to undertake the job properly (even given the recent announcement by the BMA that management costs have risen by 103 per cent over the period 1986–90, with an average salary cost of £26,000 per annum compared with an average salary growth of 2.05 per cent and average pay in 1990–91 of £35,200 for doctors and dentists); and, that NHS, once again, has failed to win public and parliamentary approval for the outcome in advance. Management will therefore find itself once again firefighting rather than re-designing the chimney and finding the right fuel to make it work, with effectiveness, efficiency and economy.

This general observation can be supported by reference to two key features in the organisation and management of health services since the late 1960s: the devolution of decision taking from the Central Department and health authorities; and, the introduction of general management within a market context. There is hardly a report or circular on NHS organisation and management over the last thirty years which does not emphasise the urgent need to devolve (or delegate: the terms are used inter-changeably) decision taking to the lowest practicable level as close as possible to the patient, nurse and doctor on the hospital ward. Indeed, the 'Griffiths Report', in 1983, argued that the approach should be that all decisions should be taken at that level, unless and until it could be demonstrated to everyone's satisfaction that particular classes of decision had to be taken at a higher level in the management chain. But, in practice, this still remains a laudable aim which has not yet been achieved, with many detailed decisions still being taken by H. M. Treasury or the Department of Health; and, many well qualified managers and other professionals at hospital level not being given full responsibility commensurate with their potential as Chief Officers. When he was Minister of Health, in 1980, Dr Gerard Vaughan, who had been a practising Consultant in Guy's Hospital, said that he was determined to reverse the management 'pyramid' by making the most senior and well paid NHS officers those working at hospital level (especially teaching hospitals in London) with those at the most junior level with least pay being employed at district, region and departmental level, in that order of authority. Dr Vaughan did not succeed in achieving this during his time as Minister; but Kenneth Clarke did 10 years later when he returned to the department as Secretary of State in 1989, having also been Dr Vaughan's successor as Minister in 1982, with the authority to approve the appointment of Mr Peter Griffiths as General Manager of Guy's Hospital Trust, with 'self governing', 'trust', 'status' on a salary larger than that of the First Permanent Secretary in the Department of Health and also the Chief Executive of the NHS.

After an argumentative start, it is now universally accepted that the general management function has proved to be one of the most important and long lasting of management changes in the organisation and management of the NHS. Indeed, it was argued strongly in the face of some of the more extreme changes proposed in the Thatcher review of the NHS, which she announced on television in January 1988 without any prior briefing or notice, that the general management function would deliver all the results required of the then Prime Minister's Review without any of the agony which subsequently was to be visited on the NHS. This same authority would argue that many of the aspects of the 'Internal Market' amount to a much too strong dose of medicine for an NHS management which has not yet come to terms with the general business requirements of the general management function. For example, a general manager who is on top of his job would be someone in whom all professionals and workers could place their 'trust'; by definition, the general manager would have 'status' in his organisation, and, therefore, he would be 'self governing', in the sense that he would be able to carry with him those for whom he was accountable as well as those to whom he owed a duty of accountability. It is therefore perfectly reasonably to argue that, left to their own devices in keeping with the first 'Griffiths Report', general managers would have been able to lead the NHS along the lines of the internal market, trust hospitals and units, consumer choice and voice and the purchaser/provider split of functions without the cost and disruption of the 'Working for Patients' and 'Tomlinson Report' reorganisations.

It is therefore important to try and see what the Secretary of State, Kenneth Clarke, intended when he introduced 'Working for Patients' and the 1990 Act. He clearly had in mind a model from the past as well as a hope for the future. From the past, he no doubt had in mind the vision of the House Governor and resident Board of

Governors in the London Teaching Hospitals before Lord Joseph's, generally now discredited, 1974 NHS reorganisation. Hence, his championing of the management and Trust Board appointments at Guy's Hospital, which took the hospital back to where it was before the 1960s and yet also offered the Minister the future prospects he sought through his 'Working for Patients' initiative. But, when you look closely at what Kenneth Clarke said in public at that time, there may be room for doubt. When he was interviewed on prime time television by Mary Goldring on the Channel 4 programme 'Answering Back' on 22 October 1989, he was asked what improvement in performance he expected of his proposals: could he give a ballpark figure – say a saving of £1.5bn from a three per cent productivity improvement each year, as a justification for upsetting so many people who seemed to be opposed to the proposals? Kenneth Clarke, with characteristic, straightforward frankness said:

> '. . . I couldn't give an estimated figure of what I think we are going to get by way of increased throughput or patient treatment . . . you may be shocked to discover, indeed you're looking slightly shocked, that we have not put together a business plan that actually forecasts improved productivity or particular improvements in unit costs or whatever, but that's just a million miles from the Health Service as it is . . . and at the moment it's got no worthwhile financial management and nobody knows what anything costs or where any of the money goes at all, so your more business-like approach will no doubt come in once we've got the new system into place and people are able to make those rather business-like judgements. . . . The BMA and the RCN, and NUPE and COHSE, and the world of DHAs wouldn't dream of asking me what I'm expecting by way productivity improvements. They tell me that's a nasty commercial judgement that doesn't apply to them. They are, I think, in difficulties when I explain to them that it will produce a much better service for the patient . . .'

Some conclusions

To return to the main theme: NHS Trusts: continuity or discontinuity? There is clearly a danger that the future will hold a series of further organisation and management reorganisations which, while in themselves continuing a trend of sorts, may also provide a discontinuity without really throwing up a new development. It is clear from the above that the overwhelming trend has been one which puts 'health status' before 'health services'; and, which relegates organisation and management to a support role. If the last 30 years of management change and turbulence are to be put to good effect, in the context of 1,000 years of health care, then the remaining years of this century must be used to build on the continuing trend. There is nothing new in 'Working for Patients': for example, even the concept of the 'Purchaser/Provider Split' was in

Barry
gone to bed

action in the 'Epsom Cluster' of psychiatric hospitals over a century ago. The 'First Griffiths Report' was the only document so far which acknowledged that it was not a case of writing new reports or prompting further initiatives or reorganisations: 'Griffiths' stated loudly and clearly (*and* in only 24 pages of triple-spaced typing!) that the task was to get action on what had already been reported, not to embark on yet further enquiry. As has been shown above, there was some form of 'general manager' in action at Barts almost 1,000 years ago! In a sense, 'Working for Patients' could violate this admirable principle of *long* standing, by causing a 'discontinuity', as people argue over the 'Status' of 'Trusts' and just how 'self governing' such new units are likely to be or should be. The challenge for Trust Chief Executives and others on the provider side, and whatever DHAs/FHSAs/GP fundholders become on the purchaser side, should be to build on the pre-existing 'continuity' and thereby minimise the potential for further discontinuity in the interests of taking health care back to its roots, in the culture and history of the United Kingdom, and yet at the same time fitting it for the requirements of the UK people, in Europe and the 'New World Order', in the 21st Century.

This clearly demonstrates also that we must build on the last 1,000 years of history in securing the best form of organisation and management to fit the health status task facing the Government and service. This is to improve the health and mental wellbeing of the people of England – the Secretary of State's personal job description drawn up by Parliament for the last 50 years. All action by government should be tested by reference to the need to fulfil this important purpose, for which, even now, 1,000 years after the opening of Barts, and before its proposed closure, we have no effective measures of output or outcome.

The job of the organiser and manager of health services to this end should therefore be expressed in terms of the key criteria identified by the foundation of Barts in the very beginning: to secure form and function of management which inspires 'Trust'; is accorded 'Status' on merit; and, is truly 'self governing' by the people giving and receiving service as well as those paying for it or standing accountable to Parliament and the people for the performance of the service as a whole.

Extract from *A Thousand Years of Organisation and Management of Health Services in the UK* by Cliff Graham, Director, Institute of Health, King's College London, 1993.

3 The composition of NHS trust boards: a national perspective

Dr Lynn Ashburner

Introduction

The Government White Paper 'Working for Patients' (1989), heralded a number of significant changes for the NHS, one of which was the change in the composition and character of health authorities. The structure adopted for the new trust boards was the same as that set out for health authorities and was styled on a model of private sector boards of directors.

An important factor which relates to the selection *process* for the non-executive directors of the new NHS trust boards, as outlined by Peck (1993) in the following chapter, was the selection *criteria*. This chapter will outline the findings of a national survey of all first wave trust directors with regard to their backgrounds, experience and attitudes. In presenting this data, comparisons will be drawn between the non-executives on trusts and those in the private sector and other health authorities; between the non-executives and the executives; and between men and women. Finally it will consider to what extent the aspirations of the Department of Health have been fulfilled and what issues this raises: for the composition of trust boards; for the background and attributes of the non-executives appointed and for the development of the board's corporate identity and influence.

The survey forms part of the 'New Authorities' research funded by the NHSTD and carried out by the Centre for Corporate Strategy and Change at Warwick University. A questionnaire was sent to every executive and non-executive director and chair of a first wave trust during September and October 1991. This was almost twelve months after the formation of the shadow boards and six months after the official creation of the trusts on 1 April 1991. The 62.4 per cent overall response rate, which included 44 per cent of chief executives, 53 per cent executives, 66.6 per cent chairs and 78.4 per cent of non-executives, is remarkable for a postal questionnaire. This survey followed the pattern of an earlier questionnaire which had been sent to every member of all regional health authorities (RHAs), district health authorities (DHAs) and family health service authorities (FHSAs) which had elicited a 69 per cent response rate.

In conjunction with the surveys, intensive case studies were carried out in seven authorities and four acute units, two of which were first wave trusts. A further two became second and third wave trusts. This study includes observation of all private and public meetings of the boards for a period of over one year. This research is ongoing and a complete analysis is not yet available. Reference will be made to the case study data where it illustrates the survey findings.

A supplementary questionnaire was sent to every first wave trust and 25 were returned. This supplement asked for general information on the selection of non-executives, the frequency of meetings and the composition of the board.

'New' style authorities and trusts

The composition of the 'new' style health authorities and trusts differs from the 'old' style in several ways. The previous tripartite system of membership comprising health professionals, local authority representatives and generalists has been replaced by one which includes executive members for the first time. Local authorities no longer have the right to nominate members and there is no obligation to include medical or allied members on RHAs or DHAs but there is on FHSAs and trusts. The size of authorities has been reduced to a maximum of 11, from numbers which often exceeded 20. With just five non-executive places remaining this marks a significant reduction in the number of non-executives (Ashburner and Cairncross, 1993).

Composition of trust boards

On the trust board two or three of the non-executive directors are appointed by the Secretary of State and two by the regional health authority (RHA), although the actual selection of all potential directors is done mainly between the region and the trust chair designate. The Secretary of State's appointments are generally referred to as the business directors and those from the RHA as 'community'. A university based non-executive is appointed by the RHA when the unit is a teaching hospital.

Of the 25 trusts that responded to the supplementary questionnaire, 12 said that the main method of recruitment for non-executives was personal contacts or word of mouth, with the regional chair carrying the most influence. Four trusts said that local business connections were their main method, which is really just an extension of the 'personal contacts' category.

On trust board four of the five executive positions are laid down by statute and must include the chief executive, finance director, medical director and director of nursing. At the time of the survey only 78 per cent of first wave trusts have appointed an executive to the fifth place. In a third of these the personnel or human resources director had been appointed. For the rest, they have either permanently or temporarily chosen to leave the last executive position vacant (Cairncross and Ashburner, 1992).

Some trusts commented on the questionnaire that the statutorily determined executive posts did not always fit with their management structure and in more than two thirds of trusts other senior managers regularly attended board meetings. The assumption in the original White Paper was that trusts would be based upon acute units:

> 'major acute units will be the most suitable candidates, but other hospitals may also come within their scope.'
>
> 'Working for Patients', p.22 (Cmnd 555, 1989)

This was the basis upon which the executive places were selected and these therefore may not necessarily reflect the management structure of community or other units, for example.

The influence of criticism of 'old' Style authorities

The new composition of health authorities and trusts with its significant reduction in the number and percentage of non-executives, was intended to change the status, role and relationship of the authority with other groups. The removal of local authority representatives raises the issue of local accountability and the removal of professional representatives raises the issue of the balance of power between the professions and management.

Prior to the reforms there was a significant body of research which was critical of the effectiveness of health authorities. Klein (1983) describes the 1948 NHS as representing a compromise between those who sought to limit responsibility to elected local government representatives and those that sought to limit the power of the medical professions. By the 1990s, with the rise of managerialism, neither group now predominates. The new composition represents the 'victory' of the argument for managerial efficiency over the representation of interest groups.

Lee and Mills (1982) criticised health authorities' lack of corporate identity as the underlying factor accounting for their failure to manage. Ranade (1985) and Day and Klein (1987), both identified a high degree of role confusion amongst members. All argued that the problems were caused by the tripartite composition where   the interests of each group of members were difficult to reconcile. Day and Klein argued that the consequence of role confusion and lack of corporate identity has been limited effectiveness and a reactive management style. The operation of authority meetings was frequently described as the 'rubber-stamping' of management decisions by the non-executives.

The new authorities and trusts, by excluding professional and local authority representation are clearly attempting to remove such confusion, and with the inclusion of executive members and the emphasis on the business sector for the selection of non-executives, to create an authority or board where shared objectives and consensus can occur.

What needs to be considered is what is being lost in this new composition, from the potential input of a wider range of professional and local interests to the lack of direct local accountability. The new composition strengthens the role of management, which by all accounts was previously secure if all management decisions were merely 'rubber-stamped', and therefore may not have been in need of strengthening.

The influence of private sector models and concepts

The impact of the *NHS and Community Care Act 1990*, has been felt in several ways. The legislation proposed the creation of an 'internal market' within the NHS, where contracts for health care could be developed between the purchasers, ie health authorities, and the providers, ie acute and community units. These ideas are drawn from commercial and private sector concepts of free competition where, as FitzGerald and Pettigrew (1991) point out, one of the roles of boards of companies is to act as the market managers. Over the first year of the reforms, however, the language of competition within the NHS was somewhat softened until general reference is now made to 'managed competition'.

Private sector models as well as concepts have been introduced into the NHS as can be seen in the composition and character of the new style health authorities and trust boards. If private sector concepts such as free competition are inoperable in their 'pure' form within the NHS (Ferlie, 1993), then it needs to be assessed to what extent the private sector board model can be adapted for use within the public sector.

Knowledge of company boards and their operations is very sparse, especially in the British context, and much of what is written is prescriptive (PRO-NED, 1987). As FitzGerald and Pettigrew show, research on boards suggests there is no fixed pattern of board composition but that in the UK there has been a general trend towards the appointment of a slightly higher percentage of non-executives. Data from Bank of England surveys show that the average size of a board is nine and that non-executive directors formed 33 per cent of the board in 1983 and 36 per cent in 1988. On these boards the majority of chairs (58%) were executives.

This presents a different model from that pertaining in the United States where 74 per cent of directors are non-executives and the average board size is 13 (Heidrick and Struggles, 1987). Here again though the majority of chairs (80 per cent) were executives.

In relation to the roles of chief executive and chair, Cadbury (1990) suggests that best practice is that such roles should remain separate. By inference this would mean that the chair should be a non-executive. In the later Cadbury Report (1992) the importance of the *independent* non-executive director for effective governance is stressed. The report recommends that the influence of non-executives should be strengthened and that the majority of non-executives should be free of any business or financial interest in the company. The evidence from the UK private sector shows that the majority of chairs and directors are executives. With just one third of directors being non-executive and one study showing that 62 per cent of these were also executive directors from the main board (Korn Ferry, 1989), then the number of independent non-executive directors is relatively small.

The new structure of health authorities and trusts with a majority of non-executives, by comparison, clearly has taken as its model an ideal form of board composition rather than current practice. Since much of the criticism of private sector boards of directors is related to the lack of independent non-executive directors and whether there is a separate and independent chair, then the composition of NHS trust boards goes some way to mitigate this.

What needs to be considered is how effective boards are in the private sector and whether the new trust boards are sufficiently different to avoid similar problems. The guidance issued by the Department of Health did not spell out in any detail what the roles and responsibilities of the board should be. Without this, it needs to be asked whether it is possible to specify the criteria for the selection of non-executives and what their range of backgrounds should be.

Non-executive director profile

Business orientation

The guidance issued by the Department of Health on selection criteria for non-executive directors was the same for trusts as for all other types of authority. If past criticisms based on the problems of role confusion and lack of corporate identity were to be avoided then there was a need for clarity of objectives. However, the criteria for the selection of directors was not radically different from those of the generalists in the past (Ashburner and Cairncross, 1991) stressing as they did that people should be selected primarily on their personal attributes, and therefore they reflect a change of emphasis rather than a total change of criteria.

Elcock and Haywood (1980) described the composition of RHAs and AHAs (area health authorities) in the 1970s as being dominated by managers and business men. The emphasis on business people was being reinforced with the intention of strengthening the management role to 'provide a single focus for decision making'. As Peck shows (1993), considerable emphasis was laid on attracting local business people.

Almost half of trust chairs and non-executive directors were employed in the private sector with a further twenty per cent being self-employed (see Table 3.1.)

Table 3.1 Present or most recent employing organisation

n=190	Chairs and Non-execs
Private (service)	28.9%
Private (manufacturing)	17.9%
Self-employed	19.5%
NHS	10.5%
Other public service	15.8%
Voluntary sector	5.8%
Other	1.6%

This represents a higher percentage of non-executives employed in the private sector than on other types of health authority where they comprise just a third. The inclusion of those categorised as 'self-employed' (19.5 per cent) would give a potential two thirds of non-executives based in the private sector. The authorities figure for self-employed is apparently higher at 28 per cent but this includes all the independent medical, dental and pharmaceutical contractors who take four non-executive places on FHSAs.

Non-executives from the service side of the private sector form a far larger percentage of trust non-executives than for health authorities: 29 per cent compared with just 17 per cent. Non-executives from the manufacturing sector form the largest category only on RHAs, at 24 per cent.

The stronger business element and private sector orientation of trust boards in comparison with health authorities is borne out by the proportion of chairs and non-executives who have had experience on private sector boards, particularly of large companies. A majority of chairs and almost half of non-executive directors had such experience (see Table 3.2).

Table 3.2   Directorships of companies

Are you the director of a registered company?		Are you a director of a company employing more than 500?	
n=205	Yes	n=205	Yes
Chair	66% (25)	Chair	29% (11)
Non-exec	44% (73)	Non-exec	17% (29)
Total	48% (98)	Total	20% (40)

More than double the proportion of chairs and non-executive directors (20 per cent) are on the boards of companies employing over 500 people, when compared with health authorities where the figure is just nine per cent.

Broadly similar percentages of all types of health authority member and trust director agreed with the idea that trusts and health authorities should be modelled on the boards of private companies, with 13 per cent in HAs strongly agreeing as compared with just eight per cent in trusts (see Table 3.3). Detailed data on health authority members and their attitudes are taken from Cairncross, Ashburner and Pettigrew (1991) and Ashburner and Cairncross (1992).

Table 3.3   Trusts should be modelled on boards of private companies

n=371	Agree strongly	Agree	No opinion	Disagree	Disagree strongly
CEO	4%	24%	12%	48%	12%
Exec	12%	45%	18%	23%	17%
Chair	5%	65%	8%	16%	5%
Non-exec	6%	59%	15%	17%	4%
Total	8%	52%	15%	21%	4%

Support for modelling trusts on boards of directors in the private sector is particularly strong amongst the non-executives. However in interviews several trust non-executives said that there were key differences between trust boards and the boards of private sector organisations. One trust non-executive who was a board director of six private sector companies, was asked if there was a comparison. She said:

'No, not directly, there isn't . . . It is the way the (trust) board is constructed, with so many diverse interests and people who do not know each other. Normally when you bring a board together most of the eight or nine know each other already'.

Another trust director explained that in his experience only people familiar with a company's business were invited to join the board. The broader backgrounds and diversity of perspectives that the trust non-executives brought to meetings was felt by many directors to be one of the strengths of the trust.

There are several factors which need to be assessed in understanding this data. Firstly, the inclusion of business people, especially those from large organisations and a service sector background (29 per cent), can be viewed as fulfilling the criteria set by the Department of Health and as being appropriate for the management of a large provider unit. It could also be argued that the general recommendations on composition, with the emphasis on business experience, favoured the operations of trusts as large employers, more than it did the operations of other health authorities who are predominantly concerned with purchasing and health needs assessment.

Secondly, the majority of trust non-executives were new to health authority membership. Here the comparison with other authorities is significant. In trusts, 73 per cent of non-executives were 'new' whereas the figure was only 27 per cent on other health authorities. RHAs, DHAs and FHSAs had chosen most of their non-executives from past members, albeit still with the emphasis on business people.

On the one hand new trust non-executives might be expected to face a much longer learning curve as they acquire the necessary working knowledge of the health service and their unit, but on the other more of them will be familiar with the role of a board member.

The wide support for private sector concepts and models is hardly surprising given the backgrounds of the majority of the non-executives. This still leaves the issue of whether private sector concepts are totally appropriate for the public sector. There may be non-executives with a wider variety of backgrounds on trust boards when compared with private sector boards, but these are predominantly from the private sector with very few from other parts of the public sector. So the question remains whether even this variety is wide enough.

Public service orientation

Despite the emphasis on recruiting directors with business experience, the two RHA appointments of 'community' directors, and some university appointments, suggested that a broader balance would ensue. In the case studies, the 'community' directors had links with voluntary or community groups but many were also in business. Similarly, some of the non-executive directors who were employed within the private sector also had other public or voluntary service experience. Thus the business element was partially balanced by a range of other experiences.

Although a high percentage of trust non-executive directors are new to the NHS, many are actively involved in some kind of voluntary activity and many hold or have held public appointments. Of the non-executive directors 40 per cent had been school or college governors, 11 per cent local authority councillors and nine per cent Justices of the Peace. Other activities that they were involved in are listed in Table 3.4.

Table 3.4   Recently or actively involved in:

n=205	
Charity	55.5%
Professional/trade association	31.0%
Church	26.3%
Political party	18.0%
Patient's group	16.5%
Chamber of Commerce	13.1%
CHC	9.7%
TEC	6.8%
Housing Association Management/Cttee	6.8%
Trade Union	3.3%
Other	17.6%

What these figures do show is that trust boards may be recruiting from the same pool of 'active citizens' as other bodies and that this supply may become more limited as the number of trusts increases. Trusts are also competing with a variety of other activities for the time that their non-executives have free from their main employment. The question of available time is an important one given that for senior people from private sector organisations in full time employment, this might be a problem. Rees (1990) found in one region that non-executives from the private sector had a poorer rate of attendance than other non-executives.

Personal profile

Age

Whereas over half the trust chief executives were aged between 30 and 44, almost 60 per cent of the chairs were aged over 60 (see Table 3.5).

Table 3.5   Age

n=367	Under 30	30–44	45–59	60–64	65+
CEO		56%	36%	8%	
Exec	1%	50%	46%	2%	1%
Chair		3%	39%	42%	17%
Non-exec		11%	56%	19%	14%
Total		28%	49%	14%	8%

Despite the age differences between the non-executives and the chairs, a higher percentage of non-executives were retired than chairs (see Table 3.6). Over 40 per cent of chairs and non-executive directors are neither in full time work nor self employed, which suggests that this particular group will have more time to give to trust business.

Table 3.6   Employment Status

n=205	Chair	Non-execs
Full time	22%	36%
Self employed	31%	25%
Part time	22%	10%
Retired	19%	24%
Looking after home	6%	5%
Unemployed		1%

Gender

Although the percentage of women on trust boards is similar to other health authorities, the percentage of non-executives is lower. Whereas 26 per cent of HA chairs and 30 per cent of non-executives are women, only 6.5 per cent of trust chairs and 28 per cent of non-executives are women (see Table 3.7). This outcome has to be partly accounted for by the emphasis in recruitment on senior business people where there are very few women, and on word of mouth contacts with the dominant influence of regional chairs who are overwhelmingly men.

Table 3.7   Gender

n=330	Male	Female
CEO	90.5%	9.5%
Exec	68.5%	31.5%
Chair	93.5%	6.5%
Non-execs	72.1%	27.9%
Total	73.9%	26.1%

The creation of trust boards has come at a time of increasing awareness of issues of equality and the adoption of goals for the inclusion of women in management and on boards, as part of the Opportunity 2,000 initiative (Ashburner, 1993). The goal for trust directorships is 35 per cent by 1994 (NHSME, 1991). This in fact represents a return to pre-reform figures when 35 per cent of RHA and 34 per cent of DHA members were women.

The decline in the percentage of women on the new health authorities was recognised as a retrograde step by the Department of Health which in the later recruitment of non-executive directors for the first wave trust boards, encouraged the inclusion of higher numbers of women. Despite considerable efforts at the centre with the support of the NHS Women's Unit, the eventual percentage was still slightly lower than that for health authorities. More significantly, only 6.5 per cent of chairs were women compared with 25.8 per cent on health authorities.

These figures did have an impact on the Department of Health as subsequent figures from the NHS ME Appointment's Unit, as of January 1993, show. The percentage of women chairs on second wave trusts has risen to 24 per cent and for third wave trusts it is 32 per cent. By comparison the percentage of non-executive directors has risen more slowly with 37 per cent in the second wave and 42 per cent in the third, but this is now well in excess of the Opportunity 2,000 goal and other health authorities.

Ethnic minorities

There are very few ethnic minority directors and no ethnic minority chairs or chief executives on the first wave trusts. The proportion of white directors is the same as that for health authorities at 98 per cent (see Table 3.8). In the United Kingdom 94.4 per cent of the population are classified as white (OPCS, 1991).

Table 3.8 Ethnic origin

n=360	CEO	Exec	Chair	Non-exec	Total	
White	100%	97.8%	100%	97.5%	98.1%	(353)
Caribbean	–	–	–	1.2%	0.6%	(2)
African	–	0.7%	–	–	0.3%	(1)
Asian	–	0.7%	–	–	0.3%	(1)
Other	–	0.7%	–	1.2%	0.8%	(3)

A King's Fund survey (1990) showed that immediately prior to the reforms ethnic minorities made up three per cent of the membership of RHAs and DHAs. Our survey showed that post reform, on RHAs the percentage had dropped to one per cent and for DHAs 1.5 per cent. It was only the three per cent representation on FHSAs that pulled the overall average to two per cent. The King's Fund equal opportunities task force and a report from NAHA (1988) recommended that involving members of black and ethnic minority communities in the planning and managing of services would result in greater equality of provision.

The then Secretary of State, William Waldegrave, said in January 1992 (The *Guardian*, 30 January 1992) that the creation of trusts may provide a fresh opportunity for identifying and tackling the under representation of ethnic minority groups in the senior management of the NHS. This represents a continuation of concern at the low levels of ethnic minorities but at the point of the identification and selection of potential directors this has clearly had little direct effect.

Motivation

The survey showed that 90 per cent of chairs and non-executives believed it was important for people to dedicate some time to public service or voluntary work. This was frequently part of their own motivation for accepting the directorship.

The public service orientation amongst trust directors is evident but they have also been identified as 'active citizens' so it is important to understand what else motivated people to accept the role as a trust non-executive. More than 70 per cent of chairs and non-executive directors saw it as an opportunity to exercise skills and experience gained elsewhere, and many others saw it as an opportunity to develop new skills (Table 3.9).

Only 14 per cent of non-executives said that the payment of an honorarium had played a part in their choosing to become a director. From those interviewed this was found to be important where the individuals main employer required recompense for time they were absent.

Table 3.9 Directorship of a trust offers an opportunity to develop
new skills and experience

n=372	Agree strongly	Agree	No opinion	Disagree	Disagree strongly
CEO	40%	56%	4%	–	–
Exec	44%	51%	4%	1%	–
Chair	16%	68%	14%	3%	–
Non-exec	15%	69%	9%	7%	1%
Total	28%	61%	7%	4%	–

A clear indication of the level of commitment from chairs and
non-executive directors is that a large majority (67 per cent) expect
to continue beyond their first 'term' of appointment and more than
three quarters expect to spend more than the recommended 20 days
a year on trust business.

Attributes of non-executives

An interesting comparison to the criteria for selection of non-
executives is their own perception of what personal qualities they
believed were important for this role. The great majority of directors
(92%) agreed that common sense and good judgement were essential
or very important for directors, with over 80 per cent believing that
they should have an unbiased and critical approach to problem
solving, sufficient time for trust business and a commitment to the
NHS. In fact 57 per cent of directors saw commitment to the NHS as
'essential' (Table 3.10).

Despite the majority of non-executives being new to health
authority membership and from a private sector background, most
still believe a commitment to the NHS is important. Such attitudinal
data can be difficult to interpret. One explanation might be that
directors from a business background are as equally committed to
the NHS as those from the public and voluntary sector, with their
contribution being one of technical expertise rather than any
attempt to change the culture. However, this commitment to the
NHS may be seen as a commitment to the new market oriented NHS.
Other attitudinal data shows that trust directors have a very strong
level of commitment to the NHS reforms, with 95 per cent of chairs
and 74 per cent of non-executives believing that the NHS reforms
will result in better care for all patients.

Table 3.10   How important to you consider the following attributes of non-executive directors? – a commitment to the NHS

n=371	Essential	Very important	Important	Neither	Not important
CEO	54%	29%	17%	–	–
Exec	66%	19%	14%	1%	1%
Chair	58%	28%	8%	6%	–
Non-exec	49%	27%	15%	9%	1%
Total	57%	24%	14%	5%	1%

In contrast to this apparent commitment to the NHS, experience of the NHS as a patient was not considered as important for non-executive directors. Twenty per cent said that it was not important for them to have any personal experience of the NHS as a patient. As with any service there are arguments which suggest that it might be useful for those at the policy level to have some experience of the 'receiving end' of services in order to properly contribute towards the setting of standards and measuring quality.

A revealing finding was that a greater percentage of directors believe it is essential or very important to have experience of management and administration in business (52%), than it is to have such experience within the public or voluntary sector (23%). This was not an either/or question and respondents could have given equal weight to both. This may reflect people's actual backgrounds and be a form of self justification but as with the support for private sector board models, it possibly shows a lack of awareness that there might be key differences in management in the public sector. It might also mean that there is a perception amongst some directors that the skills needed to run a trust are different from those needed for other areas of the public sector. How this perception develops with longer experience within the trust would be interesting to gauge, since even with the advent of the internal market, key differences remain between management in the public and private sectors surrounding issues such as service, rationing, equity and accountability.

Operations of the board

Accountability

The new composition of authorities and trusts with the removal of local authority representatives, raises the issue of accountability.

The previous membership pattern may not have produced the most effective form of accountability but it was a recognition of the importance of democratic and local accountability. This marks an important departure from long standing precedents within the public sector and it implies a radically different conception of the relationship between the public sector and local residents, from that which has traditionally pertained in the British Welfare State.

For first wave trusts the direct line of accountability was to the Secretary of State. The zonal outposts are a more recent feature having been gradually introduced over 1991 and 1992. The setting up of zonal outposts resulted from the problematic nature of having every trust reporting directly to the Secretary of State. The outposts will represent a tighter rein primarily on trusts' financial accountability. Besides the outposts there are no formal mechanisms other than purchasing contracts whereby trusts have any accountability, on a local level, to the district or the region.

The introduction of the concepts of the internal market and managed competition have made trusts more conscious of issues of secrecy, especially as regards publication of their longer term business plan. As a politically controversial new organisational form, there was considerable public interest in the first wave trusts' activities. As a consequence the case study trusts were very cautious about making any controversial changes in their first year and in the avoidance of unwanted publicity. This may have made some first wave trusts more cautious about meeting in public than in later waves when there were far more trusts and the political focus had moved away from them.

The issue of accountability has been a major concern in the creation of trusts. However the survey findings show that trust directors, like their health authority counterparts feel that they have multiple levels of accountability, both on an individual and a board level (see Table 3.11)

Table 3.11   To which of the following do you consider yourself accountable as a trust director?

n=376	CEO	Executive	Chair	Non-executive	Total
Chair	76%	73%	8%	71%	65%
Patients	48%	59%	68%	61%	60%
Community	25%	37%	45%	54%	45%
Secretary of State	40%	29%	82%	48%	44%
Trust staff	28%	54%	29%	37%	42%
CEO	–	79%	3%	10%	35%
Taxpayers	36%	27%	58%	30%	32%
Purchasers	28%	24%	47%	31%	30%
DoH	33%	29%	37%	26%	29%

These findings suggest that trust directors take their responsibilities towards patients very seriously and as a board this is matched by their acknowledgement of accountability to the local community as shown in Table 3.12.

Table 3.12   To which of the following do you consider the Trust board as a whole, accountable?

n=376	CEO	Executive	Chair	Non-executive	Total
Secretary of State	64%	80%	63%	75%	75%
Community	60%	68%	61%	60%	63%
Patients	56%	59%	63%	66%	62%
Purchasers	52%	53%	63%	60%	57%
DoH	52%	60%	50%	56%	57%
Taxpayers	36%	47%	42%	44%	44%
Trust staff	32%	47%	34%	43%	43%
Chair	20%	29%	18%	14%	20%
CEO	8%	11%	11%	8%	9%

Despite these stated feelings of accountability fewer than half of the trust boards have decided to meet in public more than the statutory once per year. In both case studies the trusts were located in local Labour controlled councils. The reaction of one was to hold a high percentage of meetings in public as a statement of their recognition of their public accountability. The other trust held no meetings in public in order to avoid attracting any form of publicity.

Individual directors may feel that they have multiple levels of accountability but their positions are not legitimised by any form of local representational links and they are, in the final analysis, only accountable upwards.

Although some trust boards have arranged regular or occasional meetings with their local Community Health Council (CHC), only one in 15 allow a CHC representative into board meetings. This is in marked contrast to health authorities where the CHC has the right to send an observer to meetings not open to the public, but excluding the private part of those meetings.

Corporate identity and board effectiveness

As outlined earlier, one of the purposes of the change in composition was to increase the level of consensus, shared objectives and corporate identity within the authority or board.

A high proportion of trust directors, 83 per cent, felt that their board had developed a 'strong sense of corporate identity'. This compares with just 69 per cent on health authorities. When compared with the wide range of potentially competing interests that had to be considered by health authorities, the objectives of the trust board are relatively focused. The stronger sense of corporate identity might also be influenced by the directors having shared the process of creating a new 'enterprise' and the higher number of directors from the business sector. There is also the important consideration that the political polarisation that occurred around the creation of trusts may well have influenced potential members who were not totally sympathetic with the aims of the reforms, against joining boards.

One of the consequences of role confusion and lack of consensus on the old style authorities was that they were accused of merely 'rubber stamping' managers' decisions. The removal of different interest groups and the inclusion of managers onto the board was designed to address this problem. The majority of directors in the survey did not see the bulk of the boards work as rubber stamping (see Table 3.13.)

Table 3.13   Do you agree with the following statement? – A lot of the work of the Board is rubber stamping managers decisions.

n=370	Agree strongly	Agree	No opinion	Disagree	Disagree strongly
CEO	4%	4%	8%	60%	20%
Exec	2%	23%	4%	53%	18%
Chair	3%	11%	5%	61%	21%
Non-exec	3%	17%	5%	51%	23%
Total	3%	18%	5%	54%	21%

The measure of influence that the board has over management decision making will need to be the focus of other studies but our survey does suggest that besides any direct influence via discussion, there are indirect factors at work. The majority of chief executives (56 per cent) and 39 per cent of executives agreed that they did not produce proposals for the board which they felt would be unacceptable to non-executive directors.

Nevertheless, whatever the level and quality of board discussions, from observation of two first wave trust meetings for over one year, it was a very rare occasion when the management proposal was not carried. The executives, especially the chief executive, sets the agenda for the board meetings and can select not just which issues go forward, but also at what point in the decision making process.

Initial analysis of observational data suggests that some items on trust agendas come at an earlier stage in the decision making process than is customary on other health authorities. This might be influenced by the relative 'newness' of the provider unit's executive to strategic management, a recognition of the value of the non-executive contributions, to the fact that provider units are nearer the 'coal face', or to the fact that they are not weighed down by the convention of past practice.

Even so, the influence of the executive directors is still seen to be dominant (see Table 3.14).

Table 3.14 Do you agree or disagree with the following statements? – In decision making, executive directors have more influence than non-executive directors.

n=364	Agree strongly	Agree	No opinion	Disagree	Disagree strongly
CEO	20%	52%	4%	24%	–
Executive	20%	54%	3%	18%	6%
Chair	3%	62%	–	32%	3%
Non-executive	10%	39%	4%	42%	6%
Total	14%	48%	3%	30%	5%

The perception of the majority trust directors is that the executives have the greater influence over decisions. Even so they did say that they were not just rubber stamping management decisions and this suggests that there is satisfaction with the level of debate. It is too early to say if the outcome represents merely a more refined version of rubber-stamping or whether the non-executives are having a real influence. The latter would appear to be a real possibility but it depends upon a number of factors. From observational data the factors which affect, for example, whether the non-executives would be prepared to go against the executive view are complex and would vary from board to board.

Issues raised

There are a number of issues which need to be considered in relation to the question of whether the composition of the trust board fulfils the objectives set out by the Department of Health. Their ultimate objective was to increase the effectiveness of boards and authorities. This was to be achieved by increasing the level of managerialism, using a private sector board model and attracting non-executives from the private sector.

In considering whether these aspirations have been achieved, the main issues that have been identified are: the composition of trust boards; the background and attributes of the non-executives appointed and whether there is right sort of breadth of experience; and the development of the board's corporate identity and what, if anything, can be said about their effectiveness. The data available cannot in any objective sense assess the effectiveness of trust boards. What can be assessed is whether the measures taken by the Department of Health in changing the composition of the boards has affected the way the board operates and the perceptions of directors.

The composition of the trust boards

Trust board composition reflects the continuing policy of increasing the influence of managers in relation to other interest groups. The creation of a more homogeneous managerially based group however, has to be weighed against the loss of a forum in which possibly competing interest groups could argue their case.

It has not been the purpose of this paper to assess the current balance of power between management and clinicians but unlike RHAs and DHAs, on trusts there was a recognition that a medical and nursing presence was required at board level. Whatever the composition of the board, there has been no real attempt to affect the existing level of power of hospital consultants.

The question was raised by community trusts of whether the statutorily laid down executive membership of the board reflected their actual management structure and needs. The assumption made in 'Working for Patients' was that it would be acute units that would go for trust status. Given that the composition was broadly similar for all types of authority, this raises the question of whether the needs of different types of board and authority should not be recognised in their composition.

The backgrounds and attributes of the non-executives

The guidelines and process for the selection of non-executives was based upon an extension of the assumption that the need for a 'more business-like service' (Working for Patients', Cmnd 555, para 8.5) meant the inclusion of business people from the private sector. Although target numbers were not specified, with two thirds of non-executives in this category this must be counted as a success.

Whether it fulfils the criteria of success in terms of the needs of specific boards and authorities is more difficult to assess. The main questions here are whether the non-executives on the trust board have the most appropriate backgrounds and whether there is the right breadth of experience. This can be judged from whether the attributes of the non-executives reflect the defined role and objectives of the board. The majority of prescriptive roles of boards are predominantly inward looking concerning the strategic and functional needs of the organisation. However, as Pfeffer (1972) points out, many boards do perform an important role in facilitating relationships with important external organisations with which the organisation is interdependent. The balance between these two needs should be recognised in the choice of non-executives.

One problem in the selection of non-executives for trust boards is that there is potentially a very broad set of possible backgrounds and experiences which could be of value to the trust and only five positions to fill. The research evidence suggests that choices made locally did attempt to reflect these needs but that the Department's guidelines on attracting people from the private sector still predominated.

The dominance of one sector in comparison say with people from other parts of the public sector or from the voluntary sector etc. may limit discussions. The data presented shows that the majority (73 per cent) of non-executives are new to the health service which results in another limitation as they need to follow a very steep learning curve before they can fully participate in trust business. Data from this research and elsewhere suggests that senior business people in full time employment have less time available for trust business and this focus in recruitment limits the number of women and ethnic minorities available for selection.

This very narrow approach, with the emphasis on business people helped to continue the under representation of women and ethnic minorities. The consequence was that the Department of Health was turning away submissions where there was not at least one woman on the board. The survey data can go some way in broadening the arguments for the inclusion of women to include positive benefits for the operation of the board, rather than just relying on compulsion (Ashburner, 1993).

The data shows that there were more similarities than differences between men and women members. However, due to recruitment processes rather than any inherent difference relating to gender, women trust non-executives presented a much broader range of experience, skills and backgrounds than did the men, who were heavily concentrated in areas such as finance, business and computing. A higher percentage of women than men had been involved in a wider range of other public service and voluntary activities. On all supplementary activities related to the trust, on average 20 per cent more women expressed willingness to become involved than did the men.

In most 'attitudinal' questions there was little difference between the men and women. On trusts 36 per cent of women non-executives felt it was 'very important' for their role to include being the 'voice of the community' compared with 20 per cent of the men. Most differences related to the degree of emphasis. Women showed greater concern about issues such as defining standards, maintaining staff morale and ascertaining health needs. Women have equal competence but a different and wider range of background, skills and attitudes.

There are several areas of skill and experience which can usefully be transposed from private sector organisations to the public. Those mentioned in the survey as being most relevant were marketing, finance and computing. However how these skills are applied in the context of a public sector service as opposed to a private sector organisation can be significant. There is a fundamental difference between operating for profit and operating for the public interest. One potential source of non-executives, senior managers from other parts of the public sector, who would not only have the necessary management skills and experience of large scale organisations but also an understanding of the implications of being a public service, were not targeted.

Corporate identity and 'effectiveness'

The ultimate test of the composition of trusts as with other health authorities, will be in their level of 'effectiveness'. It is notable that the literature which is critical of the old style health authorities does not specify in positive terms what they mean by 'effective'. It could be argued that they created an appropriate forum in which the different interest groups could argue their case. Decisions about the objectives of health care and the best way of allocating resources to meet those objectives are clearly of interest to wide groups of people and are more than just a technical management exercise. The role conflict experienced over whether they were to be agents of the Department of Health or to respond to local needs is an unavoidable problem faced by any locally based organisation responsible for the implementation and delivery of national policies and services. Reconciling the two is a very important role.

The removal of the factors which it was believed led to the old style authorities being ineffective should, in theory, increase the effectiveness of the new. Similarly when the composition of the trust boards are compared with their private sector counterparts there are key differences. The separation of the roles of chair and chief executive, the balanced number of executives with non-executives and their independence, are all in theory the factors required to increase the effectiveness of the board. Given the key differences between trusts and private sector boards, this suggests that trust boards are likely to develop a model of their own.

A higher percentage of trust than health authority non-executives felt that their board had developed a strong sense of corporate identity. This can be taken as a measure of 'success' but what needs to be considered is how this relates to potential effectiveness. In discussions and interviews with directors the key to corporate identity was seen as the high level of consensus that existed between directors. An effective board is not just dependent upon a high level of consensus but on an effective decision-making process that considers a wide range of perspectives. Consensus is more easily achieved when those with alternative or dissenting views are not included.

Several of the board's roles as identified by Peck (1993), such as asking critical questions, acting in time of crisis and assessing and even replacing the chief executive, require that the board's role is one of a potential 'whistle-blower'. The ability of non-executives to stand back from the organisation's operations can be vital and could be compromised by too high a degree of consensus. Talking of the recent West Midlands financial problems, Sir Duncan Nichol the NHS Chief Executive stated to the Commons Public Accounts Committee:

> 'Clearly it isn't enough to issue standing financial instructions. We have to make sure they are operating. . . . I feel the board did not discharge its responsibilities adequately.'

> (HSJ, 18 February 1993)

Other factors will also influence the extent to which this ultimately leads to a more effective board. These include, the non-executives' access to relevant information, the willingness of the CEO to open decision making to the board and the experience and attitudes of the non-executives.

An important consideration is which decisions are brought to the board, and for those that are, whether they are brought when they have reached the firm proposal stage or earlier when several options remain open. The latter would give the board a real opportunity to influence decision making and policy.

The research data so far suggests that the composition of the new trust boards has removed many of the factors which have led to criticisms in the past, of both old style health authorities and private sector boards of companies. What has not been established, in any detail, is what the role of the board is intended to be, against which effectiveness should be measured. The expectations of members of what theirs' and the board's role is, needs to be compared with their actual operation.

The guidelines on the criteria for the selection of non-executives from the Department of Health was very general in nature and was not based upon a clear conception of what the boards' role would be. Once boards decide what their roles and objectives are, only then can the criteria for non-executive recruitment be more precisely established.

References

Ashburner, L. and Cairncross, L. (1991) '1990/91 Health Authorities in Formation', Authorities in the NHS, Paper 3, Bristol: NHSTD.

Ashburner, L. and Cairncross, L. (1992) 'Members: Attitudes and Expectations', Authorities in the NHS, Paper 5, Bristol: NHSTD.

Ashburner, L. and Cairncross, L. (1993) 'Membership of the 'New Style' Health Authorities: Continuity or Change?', Public Administration, forthcoming.

Ashburner, L. (1993) 'Women on Boards and Authorities in the National Health Service', Women in Management Review, Vol 8, No. 1, pp 3–9.

Bank of England Quarterly Bulletin, June 1985, May 1988, 'Composition of Company Boards'.

Cadbury, A. (1990) The Company Chairman, London: Director Books.

Cadbury Report, (1992) 'Draft Report', issued by the Committee on the Financial Aspects of Corporate Governance, London.

Cairncross, L., Ashburner, L. and Pettigrew, A. (1991) 'Membership and Learning Needs', Authorities in the NHS; Paper 4, Bristol: NHSTD.

Cairncross, L. and Ashburner, L. (1992) 'NHS Trust Boards: The First Wave – The First Year', Authorities in the NHS, Paper 6 June, Bristol: NHSTD.

Day P. and Klein, R. (1987) Accountabilities: Five Public Sector Services, London: Tavistock, Press.

Elcock, H. and Haywood, S. (1980) The Buck Stops Where? Accountability and Control in the National Health Service, Hull: IHS.

Ferlie, E. (1993) 'Creation and Evolution of Quasi-markets in the Public Sector', forthcoming, Strategic Management Journal.

Fitzgerald, L. and Pettigrew, A. (1991) 'Boards in Action: Some implications for health authorities', Authorities in the NHS, Paper 2, February, Bristol: NHSTD.

Health Service Journal, (1993) 18 February, p. 12.

Heidrick & Struggles Inc (1987) The Changing Board, Boston, Report.

HMSO (1989) 'Working for Patients', Cmnd 555, London: HMSO.

King's Fund (1990) Ethnic Minority Health Authority Membership: a survey, London: King's Fund.

Klein, R. (1983) The Politics of the National Health Service, London: Longman.

Korn/Ferry (1989) International Boards of Directors Study UK, Korn/Ferry: London.

Lee, K. and Mills, A. (1982) Policy Making and Planning in the Health Sector, London: Croom Helm.

NAHA: (1988) *Action not words: a strategy to improve health services for black and minority ethnic groups*, National Association of Health Authorities.

NHSME (1991) 'Women in the NHS: An Action Guide to the Opportunity 2000 Campaign' NHS Management Executive: London.

OPCS (1991) *Population Trends*, OPCS Spring.

Pfeffer, J. (1972) 'Size and Composition of Corporate Boards of Directors: the organisation and its environment', *Administrative Science Quarterly*, Vol 18, pp 349–364.

Pro Ned Code of Recommended Practice on Non-Executive Directors (1987) London: PRO NED.

Ranade, W. (1985) 'Motives and Behaviours in DHAs', *Public Administration*, Vol 63, Summer.

Rees, T. (1990) 'Selecting HA Members: Lessons from the Wessex Experience', IHPS Occasional paper, Feb.

4 The prospective roles, selection and characteristics of non-executive members of an NHS trust board

Edward Peck

Introduction

One of the central proposals of the White Paper 'Working for Patients' (DH 1989a) was to create 'Self Governing Hospitals', later referred to as NHS Trusts. The Conservative government, a subsequent working paper argued, was 'committed to devolving decision making in the National Health Service to local operational level in order to make hospitals more responsive . . . the next logical step in the process of extending local responsibility is to enable NHS hospitals to achieve self-governing status' (1989b). Self governing hospitals were to be 'established under statute as separate legal entities . . . run by a board of directors' (1989b). This board was to have 'a non-executive chairman and an equal number of executive and non-executive directors' (DH, 1989b).

A previous study (Peck, 1991) described the influences which resulted in a mental health unit pursuing NHS trust status. The study reported in this chapter explores the potential roles of the non-executive members of the board of that NHS Trust from three perspectives: those contained in the descriptive research; those outlined in guidance from the National Health Services Management Executive; those held by the central actors in the selection of the non-executives. Following the description of the process of selection of trust board members, inconsistencies between these perspectives are highlighted as an influence on that process. The paper then analyses the characteristics of the non-executives selected for the Board in comparison with the results of the national survey of trust board membership before concluding with a review of the main issues raised.

Comparative perspectives on roles of non-executive members of corporate boards

The corporate board is a well established feature of private sector organisations which is becoming increasingly common in the public sector in the UK. There is, however, no commonly agreed approach to some fundamental issues concerning boards, such as the balance between executive and non-executive members. In this context, it is unsurprising that there are accounts of large differences in the relationships between boards and the organisations over which they preside. Molz (1985) constructs a typology of seven broad categories which purports to describe the range of these relationships.

Prescriptions for boards

There is a wealth of material detailing the roles of corporate boards, and particularly non-executive directors, in theory. Numerous books and manuals prescribe the formal duties and responsibilities that derive from statute and precedent. This material is usefully reviewed by Ham (undated). Ham summarises the theoretical roles of non-executives as being 'to bring independence and detachment to discussion of company's business . . . protecting shareholders' interests and holding executive directors accountable . . . to provide leadership in a company and to focus on strategic issues facing the business . . . bring a breadth of experience to board discussions . . . replacing the chairman if necessary.' Promotion of non-executive directors (PRO NED), an independent body founded to foster awareness of the benefits on non-executive involvement on corporate boards lists a number of specific duties for non-executive directors:

> '*i) advising the chairman on succession . . .;*
> *ii) advising on board and top management structure;*
> *iii) sing on the adequacy of financial and other information available to the board;*
> *iv) advising on the structure and level of renumeration of executive directors;*
> *v) acting as a member of a committee of the board . . .'*
>
> (PRO-NED, 1982)

Descriptions of boards

The role of the board therefore appears, in theory, to be crucial to the functioning of the organisation. For many commentators on boards, however, this appearance is misleading. Drucker (1981) observes that, 'life on the board is not juicy or exiting. Rather it is dull. Board members are more often bored by routine than stimulated by manipulating the levers of power . . . some board members, aware of their powerlessness, are beginning to complain that they serve no purpose and are kept busy with trivia'. Bavly (1986) notes that 'there is a growing school of thought which is increasingly sceptical about the efficacy of most Boards'. In the British context, Charkham (1986) concludes that 'in practice the system does not work well . . . boards are not in reality accountable to the shareholders or any one else [and] tend to be dominated by directors who also have executive duties'.

These critical views are anecdotal. Nonetheless, they are supported to a certain extent by more thorough studies where researchers have interviewed directors, usually American non-executives, to ascertain their perceptions of the realities of board life. Mace (1971) interviewed 175 American directors involved with manufacturing, mining and retail companies. He concludes that 'three important functions are performed by boards of directors:

1. The board provides advice and counsel
2. The board serves as some sort of discipline
3. The board acts in crisis situations'

(Mace, 1971)

Mace found that boards do not undertake the 'classical functions' often ascribed to them in the prescriptive literature, that is, '(1) establishing basic objectives, corporate strategies, and broad policies; (2) asking discerning questions; and (3) selecting the President' (Mace, 1971).

Lorsh (1989) conducted a questionnaire survey of 1,100 directors of major US companies followed by 80 interviews and reported significant divergence of views concerning the actual roles of directors but summarised these into 'three major duties: selecting, assessing, rewarding, and if necessary, replacing the CEO; determining strategic direction; and assuring ethical and legal conduct' (Lorsh, 1989).

Kovner (1974) analysed over 500 questionnaires returned by hospital board members in Greater Philadelphia and New Jersey and found evidence to support both Mace and Lorsh, 'they do advise and counsel the chief executive and make major decisions in the event of a crisis. Unlike Mace's business board members, hospital board members said they also do establish hospital objectives, strategies and broad policies, and ask provoking critical questions of the executive director' (Kovner, 1974).

These research findings report the perceptions of board members of the roles undertaken by the boards on which they serve. Although it is important to recognise the limitations of this research (Peck, 1993, Chapter 5), the descriptions do contain useful accounts, albeit sometimes contradictory, about the roles of board members. Overall, the descriptions do not fulfil the aspirations contained in the prescriptions.

Many writers have speculated on the causes of this gap between reality and theory. From his review of the literature Ham (undated) concludes that 'one obvious constraint is that non-executives are able to give a limited amount of time to board business, and the bulk of this time is spent attending board meetings'. Waldo (1985) thinks that the problems arise from the 'timeliness, adequacy and use of financial and other kinds of operating information' provided to non-executives and from the fact that 'most board members are nominated by the chairman or others on the board with whom they remain friends and/or business associates'. Bavly (1986) goes so far as to quote retired CEOs to support an argument that executive directors use this combination of time-constraints, information control and power of patronage to ensure that non-executive directors, and therefore boards, remain ineffective. It is apparent from the literature that the position of boards in relation to the control of the internal affairs of the organisation is at best problematic.

Pfeffer (1972) advances the theory that board members fulfil a very different set of the roles for organisations from those related to internal management. It is his thesis that 'business organisations (and other organisations) use their board of directors as vehicles through which they co-opt, or partially absorb, important external organisations with which they are interdependent' (Pfeffer, 1972). Boards of directors are, in this view, tools by which the organisation enhances its relationships with its external environment. Pfeffer tested this hypothesis by comparison of board composition and size with key aspects of the external environment for a sample of 80 private corporations. He concludes that 'board size and composition are not random or independent factors, but are, rather, rational organisation responses to the condition of the external environment' (Pfeffer, 1972).

In a further study Pfeffer, (1973) examined boards of directors of hospitals as a method of obtaining external support as evidenced by the availability of external resources to support hospital activity. The function, size and composition of 57 hospital boards were ascertained by questionnaires completed by the hospital administration and correlated with the need of each hospital to raise external resources. Pfeffer found 'that the board tended to be utilised relatively more for fund raising in those settings where the local environment provided relatively more of the resource support, while administration and technical expertise were emphasised when the organisation was not as immediately and directly tied to the support of the local environment'. (Pfeffer 1973). This research seems to confirm an earlier study summarised by Kaufman *et al* (1979) which concluded that 'where and when boards play an active role in the activities of health organisations, they serve to link the organisation to the community and the elements it possesses'.

A summary of roles from descriptive literature

This survey of the literature has demonstrated that the creation of an effective corporate board of directors is far from a straightforward undertaking. In particular, the literature suggests a variety of roles that can be undertaken by non-executive directors of boards, and thus potentially by the non-executive directors of NHS Trusts. The findings of these descriptive studies can be summarised into the following roles:

- provide advice and counsel to chief executive and management (Mace/Kovner)
- act in times of crisis (Mace/Kovner);
- assure the discipline of ethical and legal conduct by the CEO and management (Mace/Lorsh);
- select, assess and replace the CEO (Lorsh);
- determine strategic direction (Kovner/Lorsh);
- establish corporate objectives (Kovner);
- ask provoking critical questions of the CEO (Kovner);
- facilitate relationships with important external organisations with which the corporation is interdependent (Pfeffer).

There is one further research study which is especially pertinent to the discussion of trust boards. Kaufman and his colleagues analysed the backgrounds of members of 38 hospital boards and then looked for a correlation between the composition of the board and a range of indicators of the performance of those hospitals. They concluded that there was no positive or negative correlation between the occupational variables of the members of the board and the cost and quality variables of the hospital performance. These findings, the authors suggest, do 'not support the traditional contention that board members with greater expertise (financial, legal etc.) will be associated with better performance' (Kaufman et al 1979). They conclude that the way 'the board defines itself and conducts its business is more important than which occupations are represented as Trustees'.

The Department of health/NHSME's perspective on roles of non-executive directors of NHS trust boards

The problem of ensuring an effective contribution from members of health authorities to the management of the NHS is a long standing one for the Department of Health, recognised since at least the publication of the Ely Report (DHSS, 1969) and continuing through the reorganisations of 1974 and 1982. In line with the increasingly assertive managerial culture being developed in the NHS throughout the 1980s (Harrison, 1988), 'Working for Patients' (DH, 1989a) was critical of both the existing composition and role of health authorities. It argued: 'they are neither truly representative nor management bodies', and stated that if authorities 'are to discharge their new responsibilities in a business-like way, they need to be smaller and to bring together executive and non-executive members' with non-executive members being 'appointed solely on the basis of the skills and experience they can bring to the authority'. The membership was to comprise one non-executive chairman, five non-executive members and five executive members.

The model of the corporate board selected to run NHS trusts was identical to that proposed for health authorities, with the minor change of title from member to director to describe the participants on the board. Indeed, despite the emphasis on delegation and freedom, the White Paper laid down at the outset that trust boards must include 'the general manager . . . a medical director, the senior nurse manager and a finance director' (DH, 1989a). Trust boards were to have little formal room to construct the rational organisational response to their external environment described by Pfeffer (1972), either in terms of size or background of executive directors. Furthermore, two of the non-executive directors had to be drawn from the local community and all the non-executive directors were to be 'chosen for the contribution they personally can make to the effective *management* of the hospital' (DH, 1989a, my emphasis). Much importance was attached to attracting local business people onto boards, with leaflets being produced explicitly to assist in that process. The emphasis, contrary to the findings of Kaufman and his colleagues, was on the background of the individuals rather than the manner in which the Board conducted its business. This latter issue was, it seems, left entirely to local discretion.

The initial working paper on self governing hospitals specified that the board of directors 'will be responsible for determining the overall policies of the Trust, for monitoring their execution, and for maintaining the Trusts financial viability' (DH, 1989b). This specification of roles is consistent with traditional prescriptions for boards generally and non-executive members in particular (eg Pro Ned, 1982). Only one of these prescribed roles, determining the overall policies of the trust, has been suggested to be common in the descriptive research, and it is precisely the point of major disagreement between the conclusions of Lorsh and Kovner and those of Mace. Mace is clear that the 'boards of directors of most large and medium-sized companies *do not* establish objectives, strategies, and policies, however defined . . . the typical outside director does not have time to make the kinds of studies needed to establish company objectives and strategies' (Mace, 1971, emphases in original). The original Department of Health perspective focused on the role of non-executive in the internal management of the trust, and did not draw upon the points of agreement between descriptive research findings. The position of Pfeffer, that non-executive members play a major role in the relationship between the corporation and the external environment, was entirely overlooked. The roles of non-executive directors originally envisaged by the Department of Health therefore owed more to theory than practice. This narrowly prescriptive approach was perhaps understandable given the haste with which the reforms were pieced together. Further refinement was to be expected in subsequent documents, especially on a topic which had proved problematic for over 20 years.

In common, however, with much of the material which supported the implementation of the 'Working for Patients' reforms, later guidance on non-executive directors merely reiterated the original position of the Department (eg NHSME, 1990a). It was only 18 months after the publication of 'Working for Patients' that the National Health Services Management Executive issued revised information on the role of trust directors which stated that directors would be expected:

- to share corporate responsibility for policy and decision making within the trust;

- to share in the development of clear understanding of the aims and objectives of the trust;

- to monitor progress towards agreed targets' (NHSME, 1990b).

This revision focused the role of the non-executive even more on the point of dispute between Mace, Lorsh and Kovner, and, in the process, narrowed the role further than the initial prescription by removing the reference to ensuring financial viability. Furthermore, the guidance emphasised the importance of internal management in the non-executive directors role by stating that:

'non-executive directors of NHS Trusts may be involved in the work of committees or sub-committees, in particular:
(a) to hear appeals by detained patients under section 23(4) of the Mental Health Act . . .
(b) to hear staff appeals on terms and conditions of service and disciplinary matters . . .
(c) to monitor the procedures for dealing with complaints . . .
(d) to appoint executive directors and consultant medical staff'.
(NHSME, 1990b)

The published central perspective on the role of the non-executive members of NHS trusts could therefore be summarised as being narrowly prescriptive, apparently uninformed by the descriptive research on non-executive directors and overly concerned with internal management. Nonetheless, it still constituted the most detailed guidance on the overall issue of creating an effective board. It could be argued that the NHSME had focused too much attention on being prescriptive about membership to the exclusion of detailed consideration of the roles and relationships of the boards, factors which might have had more impact on the creation of a efective body.

Some perspectives on roles of non-executive directors on NHS trust boards in the selection process for Mental Health Services Trust Board

The narrowness of the role for non-executive directors promoted by the Department of Health and NHSME was not reflected in the views of key individuals involved in the selection of non-executive directors for the Mental Health Services Trust Board. The eight people represented as being most central to the selection of the non-executive members were asked to specify, 'what are the roles of the non-executive members on NHS trust boards?' The responses, which were drawn from people working at department, region, district and unit level, are presented in Figure 4.1.

SPECIFYING AS ROLE	NUMBERS OF SELECTORS
Setting and reviewing strategy of Board	5
Facilitating external relationships	4
Public relations	2
Contributing wider experience of the world	2
Assessing performance of CEO and executive directors	2
Sharing and owning vision of the trust	1
Contributing absent managerial skills/experience	1
Enhancing existing managerial skills/experience	1
Appointing CEO and executive directors	1
Valuing employees in the Trust	1
Asking questions of CEO	1
Bring to bear issues of social significance	1
Undertaking hospital managers' role	1

Figure 4.1 Roles of non-executive directors held by key individuals involved in the selection of Mental Health Services Trust Board

The eight key selectors therefore held a wide range of views on the roles of non-executive members of NHS trust boards. Nor were these views necessarily consistent between people at the same level of the organisation. Of particular interest is the emphasis on both internal management (setting and reviewing strategy) and external environment (facilitating external relationships, public relations). Furthermore, it could be predicted that the wide range of potential roles envisaged by selectors were always going to be difficult to balance in the selection of candidates for the Board, even if those involved consciously attempted to reconcile their different criteria.

The process of Mental Health Services Trust Board selection

The report, 'Working for Patients', laid down the following guidelines for the membership of an NHS trust board:

'— There will be a balanced number of executive and non-executive directors and, in addition, a non-executive chairman.
— No board will have more than ten directors, excluding the chairman.
— The chairman will be appointed by the Secretary of State.
— Of the non-executive directors at least two will be drawn from the local community . . . These two 'Community' directors will be appointed by the Regional Health Authority (RHA). The remaining non-executive directors will be appointed by the Secretary of State after consulting the Chairman. All the non-executive directors will be chosen for the contribution they personally can make to the effective management of the hospital and not for any interest group which they might represent . . . for teaching hospitals, the non-executive directors will need to include someone drawn from the relevant medical school'

(DH, 1989a).

Subsequent guidance (eg DH, 1989b; NHSME, 1990a) merely reiterated these points. The formal documents issued by the Department of Health and NHSME prior to July 1990 therefore established a narrow set of roles for non-executive directors, identified three levels of involvement in their selection (Secretary of State, region, trust chairman) and introduced the concept of 'Community' directors.

The responsibility for the selection of non-executive directors is specified as residing with the Secretary of State following consultation with the chairman of the trust, with the exception of the two directors to be appointed by the region. The formal role of the region with regard to the three remaining appointments is therefore left unclear in the initial guidance, although regional representatives were unequivocal during interviews that contact with the Department indicated that the regional chairman was always expected to submit a list of names to the Secretary of State from which his selection would be made.

The absence of detailed formal guidance from the Department of Health and/or NHSME on the selection on non-executive directors reflects much of the overall process of implementing the 'Working for Patients' reforms. The Centre was often obliged by the timescale of implementation to work out procedures and details as problems arose, particularly in relation to NHS trusts. One of the favoured methods of the NHSME seeking responses to proposals for NHS trusts was the series of NHS trust workshops convened by the NHSME Trusts Unit and attended by the co-ordinators of applications (project managers) from each of the units which had expressed an interest, and representatives from RHAs.

At the NHS trusts project managers meeting on 14–15 December 1989 it was reported that 'Regional Chairmen have been commissioned by the Secretary of State to provide names of non-executive helpers by the end of the year' (NHSME, 1989). The non-executive helper was to assist unit managers in preparing an application for trust status. This was obviously a difficult position for potential helpers as units had not finally decided to apply for trust status, the legislation to establish trusts had not received Royal Assent and the position of the non-executive helper had an unclear relationship with the position of chairman, if and when the unit achieved trust status. This relationship was described as 'murky' by one key selector and 'difficult to sell' (in a private interview).

The Secretary of State was keen to press on with the establishment of trusts and enable them to draw in external, preferably business, experience. This enthusiasm was constrained by two practical factors. The first was that the Secretary of State could not use the appropriate language of corporate life prior to the NHS and Community Care Bill, which would allow the creation of trusts, passing through parliament. The term 'non-executive helper' was therefore coined. However, the second factor was that the Secretary of State did not want to commit the Department of Health to accepting a non-executive helper as the unofficial chairman designate given the speed with which the helper was to be selected and approved. The uncertainty concerning the position of the non-executive helper did not, on this analysis, constitute a failure of conception or communication by the Department of Health. Rather, political considerations, on occasion, made such uncertainty a desirable outcome of informal guidance. The position of non-executive helpers was, at best, ambiguous. A member of the NHSME Trust Unit once remarked to project managers that they should 'treat ambiguity with ambiguity'.

This example illustrates the importance of viewing the process of trust creation, including non-executive director selection, as much a political as a rational process. Nonetheless, not all failures to unearth a coherent explanation of aspects of the process should lead to a conclusion rooted in political expediency. Nor should the impact of such ambiguity on project managers and regional co-ordinators be underestimated. In particular, ambiguity can lead to conflict.

The regional co-ordinator who attended the meeting of 14–15 December 1989 also produced and circulated notes. These have a different emphasis to the trust unit record. Under the heading 'Non-Executive Directors' they state that 'DoH regard it as important that potential candidates are identified now, especially for the Chairmanships. Trust project leaders are expected to canvas quietly and to put names to the RHA Chairman' (RHA, 1989).

The reliance on discussions at project managers meetings exposed the process of selection to a lack of consistency of interpretation between the parties involved. The Department of Health notes emphasised that the Trust Unit wanted regional chairmen to provide the names of designated non-executive helpers. The Regional notes focus on the nomination of candidates for chairman. The two activities are not mutually incompatible but they are not necessarily the same activity. Inconsistency of interpretation generated conflicts of approach which hindered the relationships between the levels involved in the selection process.

In fact, the Mental Health Unit had already located and gained approval from both Department of Health and RHA for a non-executive helper, a former DHA member and chair of the Mental Health Special Interest Group. This recommendation came from the District Chairman. The UGM of the Mental Health Unit believed that introducing this non-executive helper to consultant medical staff as the chairman designate of the proposed trust board would help achieve support for trust status as he believed that the individual was well known as a supporter of the principles and practices followed in the unit. This he did in early December 1989. Immediately, this non-executive helper/chairman designate joined the process of non-executive member selection. The UGM was explicitly clear that this non-executive helper should become the chairman (private interview).

In January 1990 the relationship between non-executive helpers and Trust Chairmanship was clarified by notes issued following a meeting of Regional NHS Trust Co-ordinators, 'the Secretary of State was looking to Regional Chairmen for nomination for non-executive helpers for Trusts. He had agreed that nominations would be informally vetted in advance of the Bill receiving royal assent. He wanted a choice of Chairmen' (RHA, 1990a). These notes make it clear that the approved non-executive helper was not to be assumed to be chairman designate as the Region was expected to give the Secretary of State a choice of chairmen. A second nomination for Mental Health Services Trust Board Chairman was therefore identified, although views varied as to how 'real' this candidate was (private interviews).

By the Spring of 1990 it was apparent that the following actors had a key role in the selection of non-executive members: Mental Health Unit UGM, project manager, and non-executive helper; district chairman; regional chairman and regional trust Co-ordinators; NHSME Trust Unit personnel. They were expected to produce a mutually agreed list of ten nominations for non-executive directors of the Mental Health Services Trust. All of them, with the exception of the Trust Unit, started to canvass potential candidates, seek the informal views of fellow selectors about their ideas, and give feedback on the suggestions of others. This reflects an openness about the process which was in keeping with the formal and informal advice of the NHSME. However, although notes of the February Regional NHS Trust Co-ordinators Meeting recognised 'the need to resolve the meshing in of nominations from Regional Chairman and Project Manager' (RHA, 1990b), at no point did these individuals operating at different levels of the organisation, and with varying views on roles, formally attempt to co-ordinate their criteria or canvassing. This contributed to the production of a complex and confused process.

Some participants in the process saw the complexity and confusion as being a necessary component of selection: 'we were arguing out the consequences in the process of implementation'; 'it was tedious, painstaking and demanding' (private interviews). Many were more critical: 'it was a bit messy'; 'it was a complete travesty' (private interviews). It was not unknown for the same individual to be canvassed more than once by different selectors or for canvassed individuals to be quickly deemed unacceptable by other selectors as 'difficult names' (private interview). Not only did potential candidates have to be initially informally checked with all the eight key selectors, but subsequently that candidacy had to be re-evaluated in the light of changing options for non-executive colleagues.

This method of locating potential non-executive directors was similar to that traditionally used for finding RHA nominees for DHA membership, only with an increased number of actors. It virtually guaranteed that the directors would be drawn from the personal networks of these actors. Furthermore, this process was taking place simultaneously with a search for candidates for the new business-like health authorities.

If selectors did not overtly discuss the overall roles of non-executive directors, then the currency of any discussion concerning conditions focused around implicit assumptions that the role was to help internally manage the Mental Health Unit, and the range of skills and interests that might be useful in that task. Figure 4.2 summarises the responses of selectors to the question 'What range of skills and interests did you decide would be appropriate for the Mental Health Services Trust Board?' Nonetheless other influences were clearly in operation. Regional officers, in particular, were concerned to pay due attention to geographical issues, the 'community' representation factor, and ensure at least one female non-executive director on the Board. The UGM and chairman designate were becoming increasingly interested in the role of non-executives as links with external agencies, and this was evidenced by their support for the proposal that the Trust Unit allow Directors of Social Services to be nominated as potential members.

INTEREST/SKILL	NUMBER OF SELECTORS
Understanding of and commitment to mental health services	5
Knowledge of business/financial issue	4
Knowledge of medico-legal issues	3
Knowledge of personnel/industrial relations	3
Knowledge of property development/housing	2
Commitment to radical reprovision of services	2
Knowledge of local authority/social services	2
Knowledge of committee work	1

Figure 4.2   The skills and interests believed appropriate for non-executive directors by key individuals involved in the selection of Mental Health Services Trust Board

The nominees to the Board

An analysis of the origin of the nine nominations eventually put forward to RHA by the chairman designate in September 1990 reveals that, excluding the two university nominees, six of the seven names originated with the chairman designate or the Unit General Manager. As the chairman designate noted, 'the process relied too heavily on people I knew'. Of these seven, all were personally known to or had been 'interviewed' by the chairman designate or regional chairman prior to nomination. The Unit General Manager personally knew or had 'interviewed' only three out of that seven. Those selectors who did not already know or 'interview' potential directors relied on informal feedback and/or short curriculum vitae to form their judgement.

During June 1990 the Mental Health Unit was completing its formal application document for trust status. The unit became aware that the Secretary of State had suggested that trusts include the names of potential non-executive directors in this application. It approached the Trust Unit to seek advice on this issue. This was some indication of the confidence of the chairman designate and UGM in the names which they had originated and guided through the informal selection process. It also illustrated their belief that revealing the people under consideration would be an asset in the discussion of trust status both inside and outside the Unit. As important, however, was the knowledge that publishing the names of the potential non-executive directors would virtually ensure the selection of non-executives from amongst those nominees. In that sense, this proposal could be interpreted as a step in the attempt by the UGM to secure the chairman and members that he preferred and thus contribute to the acceptance of trust status in the unit.

The Trust Unit responded that although the regional chairman had still 'to put forward his formal nominations for submission to Ministers' the 'Secretary of State has indicated that he would be content for applicants for trust status to publicise their prospective chairman, non-executive directors and chief executives before ministerial approval. This advice was given with the caveat that the individuals concerned should always be described as 'prospective' chairman/non-executive directors/chief executives as appropriate, to indicate that their appointments had not yet been finalised' (NHSME, 1990c, emphasis in original). The Regional response was different,

> *'It would be folly, in my view, for you to include the names of the individuals you list in your Application: however carefully qualified a description you use, it would be assumed that they will become Directors; it would therefore be extremely unwelcome if any of them were not, in the event, to be appointed. There is, as you know, some considerable risk that this might happen: and the views of the DHA Chairman and the RHA Chairman will be taken into account in addition to your own'.*

> (RHA, 1990c)

The disagreement on this point underlines the potential for contradictory advice from the NHSME and the Region. As previous research has noted (Peck, 1991) the impact on the external relationships of the unit of expressing an interest in trust status was 'profound. The unit found itself in regular and personal contact with RHA officers and Department of Health officials, and increasingly more with the latter than the former' (Peck, 1991). The Mental Health Unit therefore approached the Secretary of State direct on this issue, and a reply came direct from the Trust Unit.

This approach and response seemed to raise three issues for regional officers. The first was their concern to respect the process of selection, that is, the nomination of candidates by the regional chairman for consideration by the Secretary of State. The second was the immediate one of safeguarding the role of Region as key selectors of non-executive directors. Region did not wish to have its options restricted by the publication of names in the application documents. This implication was clearly taken by the UGM of the Mental Health Unit who, in a step clearly intended to maintain the pressure for his preferred nominations, wrote a forthright letter to Region indicating that if nominations for chairman and non-executive directors were unacceptable to unit staff then they would force the withdrawal of the application for trust status. The UGM feared that there was a cadre of political nominees without commitment to the NHS or mental health services who might be imposed on the unit. Thirdly and more broadly, this disagreement could be seen as symptomatic of a longer-running dispute about the ultimate accountability of NHS trusts. The names of the chairman designate and 'prospective' non-executive directors did not appear in the application document.

In late July 1990 the NHSME, in response to requests, issued 'a simple fact sheet on the roles and responsibilities of non-executive directors of NHS Trusts' (NHSME, 1990b). This guidance did little more than bring together previous advice, except for one section on 'The Person':

> 'Non-executive directors will be appointed to act in personal rather than a representative capacity. There are no specific qualifications for appointment. However people appointed as non-executive directors are likely to have some or all of the following attributes:
> – to have an understanding of top management in a large organisation;
> – to bring a specialist skill or knowledge, eg finance, law, contracting and purchasing, public relations, personnel, health care provision, medical education;
> – to have experience of the voluntary sector gained through membership, at senior management or committee level, of significant voluntary organisations particularly those that are community based;
> – to live or work in the area to be served by the Trust;
> – to be willing to give the necessary time commitment – a minimum of one day per month, and up to two or three days per month for non-executive directors; up to three to three and a half days per week for chairmen'
>   (NHSME, 1990b).

Once again, the emphasis is entirely on the background of the individuals. However, although it lays stress on 'management' there is no explicit reference in this guidance to the private sector. This is surprising in view of the previous enthusiasm for recruiting non-executive directors with commercial experience.

This late intervention did not appear to have any significant influence on the nine nominations for non-executive directors submitted by the chairman designate of the Mental Health Unit Trust to the regional chairman in September 1990. Indeed, the reduced emphasis on commercial experience by the NHSME could but have assisted the unit in promoting its preferred nominations. The submission lists 12 qualities, 'added value skills rather than pre-requisites' which the chairman designate said had guided the selection of these individuals. The twelve were specified as being:

1. *'the legal perspective';*
2. *detailed knowledge of the Regional Psychiatric services, ie our market-place;*
3. *knowledge of the local authority;*
4. *Knowledge of Social Services*
5. *Women/ethnic minorities − it has been indicated that female representation on the Board would be appreciated at the very highest political level;*
6. *Knowledge of nurse education and of non-psychiatric nursing in the city;*
7. *Accountancy;*
8. *Knowledge of the University;*
9. *Experience and understanding of research;*
10. *An awareness of public, private and not-for-profit sector housing − you will be aware that housing is the single most important environmental factor in precipitating mental illness;*
11. *Public relations;*
12. *General business awareness'.*

(Mental Health Unit, 1990)

This list was followed by an analysis of the extent to which nominees demonstrated these qualities. Thorough as the document appears, it has the flavour more of a retrospective rationalisation of a process rather than a description of its guiding principles from the outset. It does however indicate the extent to which the unit recognised the importance of non-executive directors as facilitators of relationships with bodies important to the Mental Health Unit. It is in contrast to the emphasis laid on internal management by the documents originating in the Trust Unit.

This letter was only in part a further component of the Mental Health Unit campaign to secure a list of acceptable nominations. More importantly, it represented the consensus that had arisen out of the elaborate process of canvassing, evaluation and re-evaluation between region, district and unit. That the nine names had largely originated within the unit could be argued to demonstrate the commitment of the region to ensuring nominees acceptable to local interests as much as the effectiveness of the campaign of the Mental Health Unit. All nine of these nominations were submitted to the Secretary of State, with the RHA choosing its two 'community' representatives from amongst them. The remaining three non-executive directors were chosen by the Secretary of State from that list.

Following the completion of the process, the key selectors were asked to reflect on which individual had exercised the most influence on the selection of non-executive directors for the trust board. Five named the UGM of the Mental Health Unit. Two, both themselves involved at regional level, named the regional chairman.

As one of the former group reflected, 'how appropriate was it for the UGM to have so much influence over the Board selection?' (private interviews). However, given that the UGM had met only five out of the nine nominees, the clear implication is that he was using his apparent influence on behalf of candidates that he did not personally know but who had been mostly recommended by the chairman designate. Two of those four that he had not met were ultimately selected.

The key selectors were asked to state, in retrospect, what aspects of the process of board formation they would like to have changed. The list is instructive and demonstrates the misgivings of the selectors, particularly at Unit level (See Figure 4.3).

ISSUE

Broader field of candidates produced by trawling wider range of agencies.

More co-ordination and clear approach between levels of organisation.

More emphasis on selecting women and people from ethnic minorities.

More formal interviews.

Less secrecy.

Figure 4.3   Suggestions for improvement to the selection process of non-executive directors from key individuals involved in the selection of the Mental Health Services Trust Board.

The composition of the Mental Health Unit Trust Board

The process described above eventually produced the non-executive directors for the trust board shown in Figure 4.4. The executive members of the trust board at its formation in shadow form in January 1991 are described in Figure 4.5.

Cairncross and Ashburner (1992) reported on the typical characteristics of board members revealed by a national survey undertaken under the auspices of the NHSTD. The characteristics of the Mental Health Trust differ from national patterns in two respects. Firstly, in the national picture 71 per cent of all directors are over 45. In the Mental Health Trust only two of the eleven directors are over 45 and the remainder are between 30 and 44. Secondly, in the national survey nearly half of non-executive directors are directors of registered companies. In the Mental Health

Trust only one of the six non-executives is a company director with the remainder being involved with public or voluntary agencies. Three non-executives are primarily engaged in working in the same university and another non-executive is a member of the Council of that university.

Designation	Background	Gender	Ethnic origin	Age
Chairman:	University Chaplain* (former H.A. member)	M	Caucasian	30–44
Non-executive A:	University lecturer in law	F	Caucasian	30–44
Non-executive B:	University professor of psychiatry	M	Caucasian	30–44
Non-executive C:	Housing Association (Regional nominee)	M	Caucasian	30–44
Non-executive D:	Director of Social Services (Regional nominee)	M	Caucasian	45–59
Non-executive E:	Accountant/ Company director	M	Caucasian	45–59

*On appointment resigned this post to become half-time lecturer in Medical Ethics

Figure 4.4 Non-executive members of the Mental Health Trust Board

Designation	Background	Gender	Ethnic origin	Age
Chief executive	U.G.M.	M	Caucasian	30–44
Medical director	Consultant Psychiatrist	M	Caucasian	30–44
Finance director	Unit accountant	M	Caucasian	30–44
Nursing director (Director of Human and Professional Resources)	General Manager	F	Caucasian	30–44
Business manager	General manger	F	Caucasian	30–44

Figure 4.5 Executive members of the Mental Health Trust Board

The second of the two unusual characteristics of the Board is a direct consequence, of the process of selection described earlier.

Given that the non-executive helper/chairman designate was chosen
explicitly because of his affinity for the values of the unit, and that it
was his networks which he felt predominated in the generation of
potential non-executives, it is no surprise that it tended towards
individuals in the public or voluntary field who could be assumed to
also share those values. The unit was undoubtedly assisted in the
selection of the non-executive directors by the guidance issued by
the NHSME in July 1990. It would be no more than speculation to
suggest that the unit had been indirectly influential in the formation
of this guidance, for instance, in the inclusion of 'top management in
a large organisation' (NHSME, 1990b), such as social services, rather
than explicit reference to private sector experience.

Conclusion

The process of selecting non-executive directors for the Mental
Health Services Trust Board was accurately described by one
participant as 'labyrinthine' (private interview). A number of factors
contributed to the complex, and confused, process of selection.

The first was the failure of the centre to take a sufficiently broad
view of roles for non-executive directors in the light of the
prescriptive material available. Second, the centre focused on
aspects of internal management that have proved controversial in
the descriptive research. Furthermore, the reluctance on the part of
the centre to give more attention to exploring the roles and
relationships of board members, was surprising given the historical
problems of ensuring that members of whatever background
contributed effectively to health authorities and their predecessors
and the range of options for board behaviour described in the
literature. The centre chose rather to focus on the attraction of
business people onto boards as in itself being the solution to the
complexities of board formation. This is not an approach that can be
assumed to be sound given the conclusions of Kaufman (1979) *et al*.
Although participants at a regional, district and unit level widened
this focus with their own perspectives, no clear agreement about
appropriate roles was ever sought or secured, even on whether the
role was concerned with internal management or external
relationships. It is clear that the UGM and chairman designate
moved increasingly to the position that facilitating relationships in
the external environment was a central role of the non-executive on
a Mental Health Trust Board. This perception of the importance of
external agencies in the activities of the unit is reflected in the report
of the IHSM on managing mental health services being prepared
whilst the selection process was underway. It identifies 'the range of
bodies which need to be involved in joint working' (Institute of
Health Services Management, 1991) as including:

• hospital and community health services;

- social services;
- service users;
- carers;
- FHSAs;
- general practitioners;
- housing – local authority and housing associations;
- education;
- voluntary organisations.

The UGM and chairman designate could not incorporate all these interests into the five available places, particularly as other selectors were stressing the importance of skills and interests relevant to the roles of internal management. Furthermore, some of these interests, eg FHSAs, were explicitly barred from membership and others, eg service users, might have constituted 'difficult names'.

This raises further issues about the nature of the guidance from the centre. It could be argued that the form of Trust Board laid down at the outset by the Department did not enable local selectors to reflect, as Pfeffer expressed it, 'rational organisation responses to the condition of the external environment' (Pfeffer, 1972). Published guidance, where it was provided, was narrow. Unpublished guidance, disseminated at project managers and regional co-ordinators meetings, was too often open to disparate interpretation, reflecting either the actual uncertainty or political dilemma of the centre, but leading to confusion and potential conflict in the participants. This was illustrated by the failure to make clear the link between non-executive helper status and chairman designate. This confusion and conflict did not create relationships where a mutual agreement of roles, criteria, candidates to canvass and assessment methods was likely.

The perceived pre-eminence of the UGM in the process, from the selection of non-executive helper through the active lobbying for inclusion of Directors of Social Services to the sharp defence of unit nominations, is perhaps the most telling part of the process. The UGM largely achieved, within the parameters laid down by the Department of Health, the chairman and non-executive directors that he wanted largely based on the personal networks of his chairman designate and emphasising a shared set of personal values. On the evidence of Kaufman (1979) and his colleagues, this might well be seen as a very shrewd way to ensure a cohesive board. In the view of Waldo (1985), it might be conceived as a ploy to ensure that the non-executive directors posed the least threat to the UGM. Either way, the perceived centrality of the UGM apparently confirms another conclusion of the work undertaken by Mace, that the chief executive 'had the power to determine the membership of the Board of Directors' (Mace, 1971).

References

Bavly, D. (1986) 'What is the Board of Directors Good For?', *Long Range Planning*, Vol. 19, No. 3.

Cairncross, E. and Ashburner, L. (1992) *NHS Trust Boards: The First Wave – The First Year* Bristol: NHSTD.

Charkham, J.P. (1986) *Effective Boards* London: Institute of Chartered Accountants.

Department of Health (1989a) 'Working for Patients', Cmnd 555, London: HMSO.

Department of Health (1989b) 'Self Governing Hospitals' Working Paper 1, London: HMSO.

Department of Health and Social Security (1969) 'Report of the Committee of Enquiry into Ely Hospital', Cmnd 3975, London: HSMO.

Drucker, P. (1981) *Towards the Next Economics and Other Essays* Heinemann.

Ham, C., (undated) *Boards of Directors: Are there any Lessons for Health Authorities* Bristol: NHSTA.

Harrison, S. (1988) *Managing the National Health Services – Shifting the Frontier* London: Chapman and Hall.

Institute of Health Services Management (1991) *Managing Mental Health Services* London: IHSM.

Kaufman, K., Shortell, S., Becker, S. and Neuhauser, D., (1979) 'The Effects of Board Composition and Structure on Hospital Performance', *Hospital and Health Services Administration*, Winter.

Kovner, A.R. (1974) 'Hospital Board Members, and Policy-Makers: Role, Priorities and Qualifications', *Medical Care*, Vol XII, No. 12.

Lorsch, J.W. (1989) *Pawns or Potentates* Boston: Harvard Business School Press.

Mace, M., (1971) *Directors: Myth and Reality* Boston: Harvard University Press.

Mental Health Unit, (1990), Correspondence

Molz, R., (1985) 'The Role of the Board of Directors: Typologies of Interaction', *Journal of Business Strategy*, Vol. 5, Part 4.

National Health Service Management Executive (1989) Notes of the December NHS Trust Project Managers Meeting.

National Health Service Management Executive (1990a) *NHS Trusts: A Working Guide* London: H.M.S.O.

National Health Service Management Executive (1990b). 'NHS Trusts: Non Executive Directors', Letter to Regional Chairmen.

National Health Service Management Executive (1990c) Correspondence

Peck, E. (1991) 'Power in the NHS – A Case Study of a Unit Considering NHS Trust Status', *Health Services Management*

Research, Vol 4, No. 2.

Pfeffer, J. (1972) 'Size and Composition of Corporate Boards of Directors; The Organisation and its Environment', *Administrative Science Quarterly*, Vol. 18.

Pfeffer, J., (1973) 'Size, Composition, and Function of Hospital Boards of Directors: A Study of Organisation – Environment Linkage', *Administrative Science Quarterly*, Vol. 19.

Pro Ned, (1982) *Role of the Non-Executive Director* London: Pro Ned.

Regional Health Authority (1989) Notes of the December NHS Trust Project Managers Meeting.

Regional Health Authority (1990a) Notes of the January Regional NHS Trust Co-ordinators Meeting.

Regional Health Authority (1990b) Notes of the February Regional NHS Trust Co-ordinators Meeting.

Regional Health Authority (1990c) Correspondence.

Waldo, C. (1985) *Boards of Directors* Westport: Quorum.

5 The roles of an NHS trust board – aspirations, observations and perceptions

Edward Peck

Introduction

There has been a considerable literature assembled over the past 25 years on the roles of boards of directors. The main conclusions of this literature are discussed elsewhere in this publication (see Chapter Four). Most of this literature can be categorised as being of two broad sorts, prescriptive or descriptive. The prescriptive work outlines what the authors believe boards ought to do. The descriptive work reports what directors on boards thought they had done.

The volume of material in the prescriptive category indicates that many commentators believe that the performance of boards sometimes falls beneath what they consider desirable or, indeed, acceptable (eg Charkham, 1986; Waldo, 1985). It is, however, the second category, the descriptive literature, which is of more relevance to this paper. Unfortunately, the majority of pieces in this literature share a methodological weakness in that the authors rely either on the accounts of directors themselves as to what takes place at board meetings or on the minutes of those meetings. There is rarely external verification of the insight and objectiveness of these participants. As Lorsh (1989) notes, 'no one, other than the directors, the CEO–Chairman and the corporate secretary knows what transpires behind the closed doors of the corporate board room'. Le Rocker and Howard (1960) in reviewing the decisions made by hospital trustees chose analysis of minutes rather than observation of meetings despite their 'awareness of the weakness of minutes as a reflection of organisational activities'. Kovner (1974) acknowledges that his study of the roles of hospital board members 'depends on trustees' opinions as to their power'. Demb and Neubauer (1992) conclude from their interviews that 'director opinions differ widely not only between boards, but also within boards'.

This dependence of research on corporate boards on two sources of data – on actors' accounts which are unverifiable and minutes which are inadequate – arises from the difficulty of accessing data from that third source, observation of board meetings. The three potential sources can be employed to validate conclusions through triangulation. Individual descriptions of board activity usually rely on only one source and this renders them unreliable.

The research reported in this chapter focuses on a first wave NHS trust board during its first 18 months. The paper reports the aspirations of directors for the board at its formation and their perceptions of the functioning of the board at the end of the period. These aspirations and perceptions are accompanied by a detailed analysis of the results of observations of trust board meetings by external observers. This material is then set in the context of the typology of board activity developed by Molz (1985).

The research reported in this paper is part of a wider study of an NHS mental health unit moving from district health authority management to trust status over a three year period (May 1989 to July 1992). A previous piece explored the decision of the unit to pursue an application for trust status (Peck, 1991) and an earlier paper in this publication, examined the prospective roles, selection and characteristics of members of the mental health unit trust board (see Chapter 4)

Methodology

The research set out to explore three perspectives on the roles of the trust board. The first approach was to collect the initial views of board members by means of a questionnaire which attempted to establish their aspirations for the board at the outset. Secondly, after 18 months members were asked to complete a further questionnaire to ascertain their perceptions of the performance of the board. Thirdly, it was agreed, with the consent of the trust chairman, to observe and record the activity and behaviour of the board over the 18 month period. An observer attended each meeting of the shadow trust and trust board and for each agenda item completed an observation sheet. Design of this sheet drew on the work of Rackham and Morgan (1977). A specimen sheet is included as Figure 5.1. In all, 15 complete meetings were observed and are included in the study. In addition, board minutes and papers were examined. The only component of board activity not included in the study relates to the confidential section of the trust board meeting. The implications of this omission are discussed in a later section.

Item No.:		Item Subject:									Item start:				Item finish:	
Activity/member	CH	A	B	C	D	E	F	G	H	I	J	K	L	M	N
												COOP 1	COOP 2	COOP 3	Other
Agreeing															
Disagreeing															
Giving information															
Questioning															
Summarising															
Challenging															
Giving opinion															
Relating experience															
Criticising															
Suggesting action															
Other															

Mode:
- Approving/accepting . . .
- Challenging/Debating . . .
- Referring on/Back . . .
- Choosing . . .
- Receiving . . .
- Setting/Deciding . . .
- Initiating . . .
- Monitoring . . .
- Amending . . .

Figure 5.1 MHU Trust Board research observation sheet

The issues addressed by the questionnaires completed by members were influenced by the previous accounts of boards discussed elsewhere (see Chapter 4). It is to this earlier descriptive work that the findings of this study are compared in order to explore the extent to which they support or challenge their conclusions. However, the questionnaires designed for this research were deliberately eclectic in drawing on published material in order to open up the areas of contention between them rather than focus on validating or refuting one specific piece of work.

The site for the research

In January 1991 the unit under consideration provided general mental health services to a population of approximately 400,000 residents in England. In addition, it provided some specialist mental health services on a regional or sub-regional basis. It had a budget of around £15 million for the financial year 1990/91 and employed around 900 full time equivalent members of staff. The district health authority employed more than 30 consultant psychiatrists to work in the unit. Although centred on a 450 bed Victorian asylum, the unit had a network of community services and significant components of the service were already located in, or planned for, district general hospitals.

The major purchaser of the trust's services was the local district health authority (DHA). It was already clear in January 1991 that this DHA was set to lose over the following years a significant portion of its annual income due to the redistribution of resources around the region as a result of capitation funding. The regional health authority had elected not to continue purchasing specialist psychiatric services on a regional basis. This enabled the other DHAs to make individual decisions about the extent to which they wished to continue their commitment to such services after April 1992. The combination of these two factors represented an uncertain financial future for the trust.

Membership of the Mental Health Unit Trust Board

A summary of the background, age and gender of board members is presented in Figure 5.2.

A brief comparison of this membership with national trends (see Chapter Three) reveals that the board was younger and that a higher proportion of the non-executive directors came from public sector backgrounds than was typical (Cairncross and Ashburner, 1992).

	Job	Gender	Age
Chairman	University Chaplain 1, 2	M	30–44
A	University lecturer in Law 2	F	30–44
B	University Professor of Psychiatry 2	M	30–44
C	Housing Association Employee	M	30–44
D	Director of Social Services	M	45–59
E	Accountant/Company Director	M	45–59
F	Nurse Director	F	30–44
G	Medical Director	M	30–44
H	Finance Director	M	30–44
I	Business Manager	F	30–44
J	Chief Executive	M	30–44
Note 1:	Resigned on appointment to become ½ time lecturer in medical ethics.		
Note 2:	All employed by one University of which E was also a member of Council.		

Figure 5.2   Background, gender and age of Mental Health Unit trust board member – January 1991

Aspirations of trust board members for the Board

In January 1991 all board members were asked to complete a questionnaire which asked two open questions. Firstly, what do you perceive to be the three main aims of the board in the first year? Secondly, what do you perceive as a major obstacle to the board achieving those aims? Nine of the 11 members returned completed questionnaires. The responses of board members to the first question are presented in Figure 5.3.

Consideration of the responses to the first question reveals a remarkable consensus of view amongst members as to the need to overcome the negative impact of the creation of the trust and trust board. Six of the respondents included responses in this area (allay anxieties about trust status; gaining respect of staff; raising morale). Much of this impact was perceived to be on the staff of the trust, symbolised by the result of the staff ballot which recorded 80 per cent opposition to the trust on the ballot papers returned. It is reasonable to expect from this that the board would be conscious of the image it presented, and the messages that its decisions conveyed, to staff in the unit. It is surprising that the more apparently obvious responses (eg create clear corporate view of function/role of board; establish effective strategic decision making) did not occur more frequently. This may reflect the lack of experience of board members of commercial board life.

	Executive Directors	Non-Executive Directors
Create clear corporate view of function/role of board	2	2
Allay anxieties about trust status (stability)	3	
Establish effective strategic decision making	1	2
Gaining respect of staff		2
Achieve improvements in users lives	2	
Determine value base, aims, objectives	1	1
Creating culture of change	1	
Secure contracts (quality/resources)	1	
Opportunity for users to influence decision making	1	
Optimise land sale	1	
Clear basis for relationship with Purchaser	1	
Establish relationships between board and other groups in unit	1	
Understand trust		1
Prioritising issues		1
Raising morale		1
Do no harm		1

Figure 5.3 Executive and non-executive directors aims for the board in the first twelve months

Review of the responses to the second question indicate the extent to which members appeared to believe that the obstacles to achieving these aims lay outside of the board and therefore beyond its control (see Figure 5.4). Of the nine responses, only three (lack of common value base; lack of faith on board's behalf; failure to gel as a team) placed the obstacles under the control or direct influence of the board itself. The remainder locate the obstacles wholly (or in one case partially) outside of the board and the trust, in two cases relating to quite technical issues (problems relating to conveyance of assets to trust; cost of service allocation) but in three instances referring to the volatility of the environment in which trusts were being created (unstable outside environment; NHSME/RHA struggle over trust empowerment; role uncertainty due to undue outside interference). In these circumstances of perceived threat, it is possible that the board will have a tendency to view the external world with some suspicion.

Executive Directors

- Problems relating to conveyance of assets to trust
- Unstable outside environment
- Cost of service allocation
- Lack of common value base
- NHSME/RHA struggle over trust empowerment
- Politicians

Non-Executive Directors

- Fear associated with change
- Lack of faith on Board's behalf
- Failure to gel as a team
- Role uncertainty due to undue outside interference

Figure 5.4   Executive and non-executive directors' perceptions of major obstacles to achieving aims in first twelve months.

Overall then, responses to these two questions seem to indicate that the trust board at its outset represented a body with pressures on either side. On the one hand, it had as a major aim the task of overcoming staff anxieties about the creation of the trust which had brought the board into existence. On the other hand, this aim had to be achieved in the context of an uncertain, uncontrollable and potentially threatening outside world.

In addition to these two questions addressed to all members, non-executive directors were asked one further open question: why do you think that you were approached to be a board member? The responses are summarised in Figure 5.5.

The most recurrent theme suggested by the five non-executive directors who responded was that their personal value base would fit with that of the Mental Health Unit ('Chairman thought I would fit in'; 'sympathy with top management ethos'; personal philosophy). In light of the research on the selection of the trust board (see Chapter Four) this should come as no real surprise as that work concluded that the UGM 'largely achieved, within the parameters laid down by the Department of Health, the chairman and non-executive directors that he wanted primarily based on the personal networks of his chairman designate and emphasising a shared set of personal values'.

- Financial knowledge
- Commercial experience
- Chairman thought I would fit in
- Sympathy with top management ethos
- Common sense
- Reliability
- Relevance of jobs in field
- Range of local/regional contacts
- Personal philosophy
- To give choice of academic to Secretary of State

[n=5]
Respondents asked to specify their understanding of reason for approach

---

Figure 5.5 The reason why non-executive directors felt that they had been approached to be on the board.

The further implication is that not only were the non-executive directors predominantly chosen on the basis of their personal beliefs but that the knowledge of those beliefs was rooted in the personal and professional relationships with the chairman designate. As that individual stated, "the process relied too heavily on people I knew" (Peck, 1993) and, as has already been noted, four of the six non-executive directors either worked in or were involved in the management of the same university. The two non-executive directors not connected with that university were managers in public sector organisations. All of the non-executive directors could, therefore, be expected to be sympathetic to the public service values of the trust expressed in its application for trust status (Mental Health Unit, 1990). The benefit of such a group might be that it would grow quickly into a cohesive board focused around a set of shared values. The disadvantage might be that there would be too little challenge to the consensus views that such a group might readily adopt.

Finally, non-executive directors were asked to indicate their perception of the importance of a number of suggested roles that could be adopted by the board. The responses of the non-executive directors are recorded in Figure 5.6.

The options offered to the non-executive directors were drawn from amongst the roles described in the work of Mace (1971), Kovner (1974), and Lorsh (1989) augmented by the views of their selectors (Peck, 1993). The five non-executive directors who responded highlighted five roles as being particularly important: setting and reviewing overall strategy for the trust; ensuring ethical and legal

	Very important	Important	Useful	Marginal	Not appropriate
(a) Setting and reviewing overall strategy for the Trust	1111	1			
(b) Ensure ethical and legal conduct by the Executives	1111	11			
(c) Sharing and owning the mission/vision of the Trust	1111	1	1		
(d) Assessing performance of Executive members	11	111			
(e) Contributing skills/experience which would otherwise be absent from the Trust	111	1	1		
(f) Appointing Executive members	1	111		1	
(g) Acting in time of crisis	1	111		1	
(h) Asking provoking critical questions of the Chief executive	1	11	11		
(i) Giving legitimacy to and enabling Executives to fulfil their roles	11	1	1	1	
(j) Facilitating relationships with external agencies on behalf of the Trust	1	111	1		
(k) Bringing to bear issues of broader social significance on the Trust	1	11	1	1	
(l) Valuing staff in Trust	11	11			
(m) Public relations role on behalf of Trust	1	1	111		
(n) Enhancing existing skills/experience in Trust		1111			
(o) Fulfilling 'hospital managers' role			1	111	1
other: Please specify					

Figure 5.6 The importance attached to potential roles for the board by non-executive directors.

conduct by the executives; sharing and owning the mission of the trust; assessing performance of executive members; contributing skills/experience which would otherwise be absent from the trust. Interestingly, these priorities to a large extent mirror the major roles which emerge from US directors described in the Lorsh (1989) study, 'selecting, assessing, rewarding and, if necessary, replacing the CEO; determining strategic direction; and assuring ethical and legal conduct'. The emphasis on policy is also consonant with the advice issued by the NHSME (1990) although in other respects these non-executives take a broader view of the role of directors.

That the non-executives attribute importance to 14 of the 15 roles suggested to them could imply either a lack of focus or beginner's enthusiasm, or both. It is significant to note that the roles associated with the outside environment (public relations role on behalf of trust; facilitating relationships with external agencies on behalf of trust) are viewed as less important than a number of roles connected with the internal governance of the trust. In this respect, the non-executive directors are demonstrating a different perspective from that held by those responsible for their selection.

The conduct of the Trust Board

In February 1992 the shadow board agreed standing orders that defined the formal procedures of the board. One of the key features included in these standing orders was the decision to make all the monthly meetings open to the public, except when the board saw reason to exclude them. Further, the board undertook to co-opt representatives from the consumer council, voluntary sector advisory group and community health council as speaking but non-voting members. Both of these features represent practical manifestations of a genuine aspiration to ensure openness about the operation and decisions of the board. In common with many boards, a number of sub-committees were established comprising board members and representatives drawn from unit staff and the consumers council. Initial sub-committees covered quality control, ethics, research, and capital planning.

Informal issues, such as the attitudes adopted by the chairman and by directors were as important to the conduct of the meetings as the formal arrangements. Three examples will have to serve to illustrate the people-centred approach which characterised most meetings. Firstly, the chairman started each meeting with a one minute silence so that members could clear their minds in order to focus on the business in hand. Secondly, the most common entry in the 'other' category on the observation sheet was 'joke'. Thirdly, during the course of one board meeting a non-executive director served coffee to members of the public.

Observations of the NHS trust board

This section will present a summary of the data collected on the observation sheets. It is important to stress that the observation data is suggestive rather than definitive and open to differing interpretations. One interpretation will be developed.

Firstly, the total number of contributions made at each Board meeting by each participant was calculated, along with the average contribution per meeting attended (see Figure 5.7). The chairman (CH) predictably stands out as the major contributor, with over twice as many contributions to the discussion as the next most significant contributor, the chief executive (J). More detailed analysis reveals that almost half (841) of the total number of contributions could be characterised as 'giving information' and that this was the major activity undertaken by both chairman and chief executive. However, the overall balance of contributions, 1,057 by non-executives and 706 by executives, seems to demonstrate a healthy equality between members, although much of the non-executive activity was asking questions which were then addressed by the chair, chief executive or business manager (I).

Closer inspection of these data reveals some interesting trends within this overall balance. Firstly, amongst the non-executives, Directors D and B made the highest number of contributions. As Director of Social Services, Director D had professional experience and expertise in the field of the trust's activities. Furthermore, he was used to being accountable as a public sector manager to a committee charged with overseeing the work of his department. Similarly, Director B, the university professor of Psychiatry, possessed specialised knowledge about the unit's services. In addition, he carried a brief to represent the interests of the university, particularly the academic department of Psychiatry, at board meetings. It is perhaps, therefore, not surprising to find that they have the most to contribute. Furthermore, there is no discernable trend over time in the number of contributions made by Director B at meetings. This analysis is more difficult to undertake for Director D because he was absent from the final four meetings observed.

The importance of the knowledge possessed by Directors B and D comes into clearer focus when we consider activity defined as challenging. Only 34 contributions were felt to warrant this description during the 15 meetings observed. Half of these contributions were made by Directors B and D; eight by Director B and nine by Director D.

In contrast, Director A had no such direct involvement in the work of the Unit. She was, therefore, largely reliant on board papers and discussions for her understanding of the unit. As might have been predicted, there is evidence that her number of contributions per meeting was increasing over time. Furthermore, it would appear that

Member	CH	A	B	C	D	E	F	G	H	I	J	K	L	M	N	Total
Total	558*	73	114	83	112	117	49	83	113	177	236	48	59	14	195	1928
Average per meeting	32*	6	9	7	12	9	4	6	8	12	16	4	5	2	12	
No of meetings attended	14	11	12	12	9	12	11	12	13	13	12	10	10	7	12	

Note: Participant K = CHC Rep
Participant L = Consumer Council Rep
Participant M = Voluntary Services Advisory Group Rep
Participant N = Other

*If the introductory remarks to each item are discounted, along with items where only the Chairman contributed, then this figure is reduced to 381. The average number of contributions is reduced to 27.

Figure 5.7 Total number of contributions made by each participant and average number of contributions made by each participant

towards the end of the observation period she was more likely to suggest action for the Board as well as to ask questions and give opinions. In this respect, Director A seems to demonstrate the learning curve of a non-executive director on entering an organisation of which she has little prior knowledge, particularly one with limited experience of corporate board activity. This is in contrast to Director E who, although possessing little prior knowledge of the services provided by the unit, did have experience of corporate board life. Director E was a consistent contributor to Board discussion from the beginning. With regard to executive directors, it is notable that the two directors from the professions (F – nurse director; G – medical director) made the lowest average number of contributions. It is difficult to conclude whether these lesser quantities of intervention were a consequence of position or personality. With regard to the nurse director, her post as Director of Human and Professional Resources contained a brief to speak on behalf of all non-medical professions, not just nursing, and to deal with personnel issues. This combination of responsibilities would suggest that a significant number of agenda items would fall at least partially within her curtilage. It is possible to speculate that one factor restricting her contribution may have been the consequence of the traditional status of nursing amongst the mental health professions.

The position with regard to the medical director is perhaps more clearly structural than personal. The medical director was appointed to the Board to participate in the corporate decision making of that board. At the same time, he was chosen because he was the Unit Medical Representative with a responsibility to represent the views of doctors to management. He was, therefore, expected to play a management role in respect of the same individuals whom he was expected to represent. This is clearly a difficult balance of expectations. In practice, Director F largely restricted his activities to giving information and questioning.

Secondly, the total number of agenda items considered by the Board were analysed by mode of activity and category of activity (see Figure 5.8). The mode of activity was recorded on the observation sheet (see Figure 5.1) and each item could be allocated to one of nine types. The categories of Board activity were devised following the completion of the observations and each item could be allocated to one of 12 categories.

The most common mode of activity for the Board was 'receiving' (reports, papers) with well over half of the items being characterised as belonging within this mode. The only other mode of activity which reached double figures was 'approving'. In terms of the category of activity, the single largest number of items related to board procedure (largely apologies for absence and approving minutes), followed by trust procedure, external relationships, implementation (of strategy) issues and trust policy/plans. This

Mode Category	Approving	Choosing	Setting	Monitoring	Challenging	Receiving	Initiating	Amending	Referring back	Total
Board procedure	19 (4)	2				17 (2)		1		39 (11)
Trust procedure	10		2		2	5		1	1	21
Trust policy/plans	2				1	10		1		14
Trust objectives	2							1		3
Implementation issues	7					10				17
Financial issues	3					9				12
Incident report						2				2
Trust mgt. initiatives	2					5		1		8
External relationships	2		1		1	17		1	1	23
Personnel info/issues	1					3				4
Response to national initiatives	2					6				8
Internal mgt. issues	2					1				3
Total	52 (38)	2	3	–	4	85 (71)	–	6	2	154 (126)

Note: Figures in brackets discount receiving apologies for absence and approving minutes of previous meeting.

Figure 5.8 Total number of agenda items analyzed from observation data by mode of board activity and category of board activity.

seems an appropriate mix given the aims of all of the directors and the roles selected by the non-executives. This analysis of category and mode of activity correlates closely with a separate analysis based on examination of board minutes.

More revealing than the analysis of the number of agenda items in each mode and category is the time spent discussing these agenda items, again analysed by mode and category of activity (see Figure 5.9). Of the 1,757 minutes that the 15 observed Board meetings were in session, almost two thirds were characterised as being spent in the receiving mode. A total of 368 minutes were spent in discussion characterised as fitting the approving mode. In relation to the categories of Board activity, almost one third of Board time was taken up in discussing trust policy/plans. This category of activity took almost twice as long as the category that took up the second single largest amount of time, external relationships. Once again, it would appear that the Board was spending its time addressing the right issues in order for directors to fulfil their aims and roles for the Board.

It is, however, important to consider the category and mode simultaneously. It is undoubtably true that the Board was spending its time addressing trust policy/plans and external relationships. But for the majority of the time that it was addressing these issues it was receiving information about them from executive directors or other trust employees. The role relating to trust policy/plans envisaged the Board setting and reviewing rather than merely receiving. It could be argued that receiving is a passive mode of activity. If this argument is accepted, then over 60 per cent of the overall observed trust board activity was of a passive nature, with over 85 per cent of the time spent addressing trust policy/plans being passive.

The time spent in approving mode involved the board in approving recomendations from executive directors and other trust employees, primarily on trust objectives, trust procedure and board procedure. This mode was influenced by the style of board papers, examination of which reveals that they mostly consisted of a description of the problem or issue which led into the reccomendation. Rarely did papers contain alternative perspectives or options for choice.

Perceptions of board members after 18 months

In May 1992 all board members were asked to complete a questionnaire which included the following four questions:

- What do you perceive to be the major achievements of the Trust Board during the past 12 months?

- Which three roles do you feel the Board have been most successful at undertaking during the past 12 months?

Mode / Category	Approving	Choosing	Setting	Monitoring	Challenging	Receiving	Initiating	Amending	Referring back	Total
Board procedure	61	8			18		40			127
Trust procedure	76		23		37	13		17	11	177
Trust policy/plans	13				38	444		10		505
Trust objectives	92							23		115
Implementation issues	45					121				160
Financial issues	19					97				116
Incident report						10				10
Trust mgt. initiatives	22					41		19		82
External relationships	8		12		10	195		40	2	267
Personnel info/issues	2					12				14
Response to national initiatives	11					31				44
Internal mgt. issues	19					127				146
Total	368	8	35		85	1099		149	13	1757

Figure 5.9 Total length of meetings in minutes analyzed from observation data by mode of board activity and category of board activity.

- What have been the major obstacles to the Board's effectiveness?
- What have been the three major issues facing the trust during the past 12 months and what has the contribution of the Board to these issues been ie critical, useful, or marginal?

A summary of the responses from the seven board members who replied are presented in Figures 5.10, 5.11, 5.12 and 5.13. It is illuminating to compare Figure 5.10 with Figure 5.3. The major achievements perceived by board members during the first 12 months of the existence of the Board bear little resemblance to the aims that those same members had for the Board at its outset. Overall, the aims could be described as being conceptual and intangible whereas the achievements could be described as being practical and tangible. Nonetheless, it appears possible to establish some connection between the aims (eg gaining respect of staff) and achievements (eg commitment to Equal Opportunities Policy). However, it is surely significant that there is no achievement which seems to connect with the aim of creating a clear corporate view of the function and role of the Board.

	Executive Directors	Non-Executive Directors
Commitment to equal opportunities policy	2	1
Controlled capital programme whilst allowing flexibility and speed of decisions.	2	
Met 3 financial objectives of Trust as laid down by NHSME.	2	
Commissioning organisational review.		2
Overseeing smooth transition to Trust status.		2
Getting known for openness.		2
Public Forum with increasing ability to debate openly.		1
R & D funding for use in Trust.	1	
Established role and general credibility with staff.	1	
Financial prudence		1
Balance between development and coordination.		1
Met all key objectives and reviewed them.	1	
Note: Respondents asked to specify three major achievements.		

Figure 5.10   Trust board members perceptions of the three major achievements of the board during the first twelve months

		Executive Directors	Non-Executive Directors
(a)	Sharing and owning the mission/vision of the Trust.	2	2
(b)	Setting and reviewing overall strategy for Trust.	2	
(c)	Contributing skills/experience which would otherwise be absent from the Trust.	4	
(d)	Enhancing existing skills/experience in Trust.	1	1
(e)	Public relations role on behalf of Trust.		
(f)	Fulfilling 'hospital managers' role.	2	
(g)	Appointing Executive members	1	1
(h)	Assessing performance of Executive.		
(i)	Acting in time of crisis.		
(j)	Giving legitimacy to and enabling Executives to fulfil their roles.		3
(k)	Facilitating relationships with external agencies on behalf of the Trust.	3	1
(l)	Bringing to bear issues of broader social significance on the Trust.	1	3
(m)	Valuing staff in Trust.		2
(n)	Asking provoking critical questions of the Chief Executive.		
(o)	Ensure ethnic and legal conduct by the Executives.		
Other:			
	Academic advice.		1
	Corporate development role.	1	
	Clinical advice.		1
	Occasional happiness.		1
Key: Respondents asked to choose three from list offered			

Figure 5.11   Trust board members were asked to indicate which three of the roles did they believe the Board had been most successful at undertaking during the previous twelve months

A comparison of Figure 5.11 and Figure 5.6 demonstrates the extent to which trust board members believe that the Board had successfully undertaken the roles which seemed appropriate at the outset. Most strikingly, only two directors felt that amongst the three most successful roles that the Board had undertaken had been the setting and reviewing of overall strategy for the trust. Furthermore, no trust board members felt that the Board could number amongst its three most successful roles the assessment of the performance of the executive members.

- Public Meetings (2)

- Lack of time (2)

- Lack of information

- Political uncertainty

- Unconscious desire of Executive Directors to bypass Board

- Lack of involvement in preliminary strategy and planning

- Not in touch with real issues/problems

- Initially lacking mutual trust and understanding

Figure 5.12   Trust board members were asked to indicate what had been the major obstacles to the Board's effectiveness.

The major obstacles which had impeded the work of the Board (see Figure 5.12) turned out to be far more practical and under the control of the Board itself than those predicted in January 1991 (see Figure 5.4). Initially, no director had identified lack of time or the public nature of board meetings as being an obstacle to the functioning of the Board. These practical and largely internal obstacles seemed to have replaced the external threats envisaged by members in January 1991.

Perhaps the most telling information is contained in Figure 5.13. Of the major issues faced by the trust during the previous 12 months, less than half of the contributions of the Board were perceived to be critical or useful to these issues. Over half of the contributions of the Board on these issues were reported as being marginal. Even where the contribution of the Board was perceived by one member as being critical, another member perceived the contribution of the Board on that same issue as being marginal. Notwithstanding the wide differences of view between members with regard to the same issue, it is difficult to avoid the conclusion that the contribution to the Board on the major issues facing the trust had been marginal rather than useful. It is surely significant that board members were able to recognise the major issues that they felt were impacting upon the trust even though these issues were either not being discussed at the board meetings or not addressed in an appropriate fashion to enable the Board to play a key role. The implication is, of course, that these major issues were either not being addressed or, more likely, were being handled outside of the Board.

	Critical	Useful	Marginal
Obtaining sufficient income and achieving financial targets	1	1	1
Contracts for services	1	1	1
Community care		1	1
Service development			2
Matching capital programme to available resources		1	
Capital changes in programmes on buildings			1
Staff development			1
Establishing viable organisation		1	
Developing or taking forward strategy			1

Note: Respondents asked to specify issues and rate Board contribution

Figure 5.13   Trust board members were asked to indicate what had been the three major issues facing the Trust during the previous twelve months and what the contribution of the board to each of these issues had been ie. critical, useful or marginal.

The private sessions of the board meetings

The private sessions of the Board were not observed. In its standing orders, the Board expected that 'as a general guide exclusion would be expected when:

(a) *Matters related to individual patients and members of staff are discussed;*
(b) *Detailed matters relating to proposals for the placing of contracts (as opposed to, say, the underlying strategic aims) are discussed;*
(c) *Instructions are made with a guide to legal action by the Trust'.*

It is not known the extent to which these remained the criteria for items being placed on the private part of the agenda. Nonetheless, it appears that the financial performance and capital programme of the trust became major themes during private sessions. The former theme would presumably have focused the attention of directors on the internal management of the trust. The latter theme would presumably have focused the attention of directors on the policy/plans of the trust. It is possible, therefore, that the analysis undertaken in previous sections underestimates the amount of time spent by directors in these categories of activities. It is impossible to speculate on the mode of activity during these private sessions.

The board of directors in the first 18 months

In the second questionnaire, directors were asked to state the three roles which they believed the Board had been most successful in fulfilling. There is, however, broad compatibility between the aspirations and the perceptions, although two items, 'facilitating relationships with external agencies on behalf of the trust' and 'bring to bear issues of broader social significance on the trust' seem to have taken a higher priority than was originally envisaged. There is one important exception. Although originally the most important potential role, 'setting and reviewing overall strategy of the trust' was perceived to have been fulfilled by the trust board by only two directors. The importance of this is that it supports the position of Mace (1971) who concluded from his research that boards do not undertake the role of 'establishing basic objectives, corporate strategies, and broad policies'.

The evidence of the observation data suggests that most directors were correct not to include 'setting and reviewing overall strategy for the trust' as one of the major roles fulfilled by the board. Of the 505 minutes that the board spent considering trust policy/plan, over 85 per cent of them were spent in the passive activity of receiving information. Nonetheless, board directors chose other roles in which they felt the board had been more successful. However, these views need to be seen in the context of the perception that the contribution of the board to the key issues facing the trust had been marginal rather than central or useful. This conclusion concurs with the overall picture arising out of the observation data which suggests that over 60 per cent of the time spent by the board was in receiving mode which is argued to be a basically passive state.

This conclusion is important. When asked to comment upon the roles that they had undertaken, the directors on the trust board made a selection. From this, one might assume that they felt their contribution had been an important one. However, when asked directly about the value of their contribution a very different picture emerges which is in keeping with the conclusions of the observation of the Board.

It might be suggested that the conclusions about the trust board are specific to a board during its initial phase. This line of argument is somewhat undermined by the observation data on the final meeting observed where over 90 per cent of the duration of the meeting was spent in receiving mode.

Where would the board fit into a typology of boards

One of the most useful typologies developed to analyse the role of the board of directors is that of Molz (1985). Molz suggests a

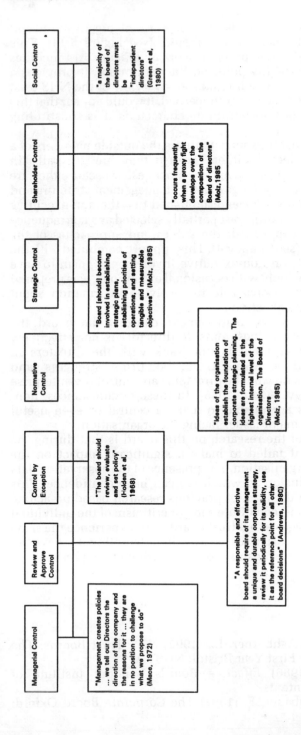

Figure 5.14 Continuum of board of directors; organisation and control

continuum between seven discernable sorts of organisation and control exhibited by boards of directors (see Figure 5.14). This typology itself builds upon previous work and Figure 5.14 includes definitions of each staging point on the continuum. It provides a broad framework with which to take an overview of the NHS trust board with which we have been concerned. It would appear that this board is at the end of the continuum characterised as constituting managerial control.

Molz maintains that 'in such situations the outside members of a board are often selected either because they are generally in agreement with existing management practices, or because they are viewed as unlikely to challenge existing management structure and legitimacy'. It has already been established that the non-executive directors of the trust were at least partially selected as a consequence of their perceived support for the values and approaches of the Mental Health unit (see Chapter 4). This support, combined with the practical constraints on non-executive involvement, seem to have resulted in a board which, with occasional exceptions, was prepared to accept a largely passive role in receiving information about managerial and clinical activity.

Molz continues 'where management controls the board the valuable experiences of these outside directors is not effectively utilised . . . If management is not frank with the directors in conveying internal assessment of the firms strengths and weaknesses, there is no way the directors can control the enterprise or corporate strategy' (Molz, 1985). In these circumstances, non-executive directors are unable to make a central or even useful contribution to the major issues facing the organisation.

The conclusion of the research on this board is that during the initial 18 months it failed to make a significant impact on the governance of the organisation. The presence of the observation data makes this a conclusion in which we can have confidence. This failure does not, in the light of previous research based on actors' accounts and minutes, constitute a major criticism of the individual board. Rather, it suggests that trust boards will experience the same problems as other corporate boards in attempting to have an effective impact on the organisations over which they preside.

References

Cairncross, L. and Ashburner, L., (1992) *NHS Trust Boards: The First Wave* – The First Year Bristol: NHSTD.

Charkham, J.P. (1986) *Effective Boards* London: Institute of Chartered Accountants.

Demb, A. and Neubauer, F. (1992) *The Corporate Board* Oxford: OUP.

Kovner, A.R. (1974) 'Hospital Board Members and Policy-Makers: Role, Priorities and Qualifications', *Medical Care*, Vol XII, No. 12.
Le Rocker, F.C. and Howard, S.K. (1960) 'What Decisions Do Trustees Actually Make?', *The Modern Hospital*, Vol 94, No.4
Lorsch, J.W. (1989) *Pawns or Potentates* Boston: Harvard Business School Press.
Mace, M. (1971) *Directors: Myth and Reality* Boston: Harvard University Press.
Mental Health Unit (1990) Application for NHS Trust Status
Molz, R., (1985) 'The Role of the Board of Directors: Typologies of Interaction', *Journal of Business Strategy*, Vol 5, Part 4.
Peck, E. (1991) 'Power in the NHS – A Case Study of a Unit Considering NHS Trust Status', *Health Services Management Research*, Vol 4, No.2
Peck, E. (1993) 'The Prospective Roles, Selection and Characteristics of Non-Executive Members of an NHS Trust Board' in Peck, E. and Spurgeon, P. *NHS Trusts in Practice* London: Longman.
Rackham, N. and Morgan, T. (1977) *Behaviour Analysis in Training* London: McGraw Hill
Waldo, C.N. (1985) *Boards of Directors* Westport: Quorum.

6 NHS Trusts – Purchaser perspectives

John Dennis

Purchaser perspective A

In writing this perspective I am aware that I can be labelled 'a poacher turned gamekeeper' having relatively recently made the change from 'purchaser' to 'provider'. As one for whom both the purchasing and providing function is of great interest I hope that the dual experience can offer balance rather than bias. If I was to be allowed a degree of bias resulting from the change, it would be that the trust as a provider bears an enormous share of the risks which I believe will be a major factor in the significant changes in trust structure which will emerge within the next five years.

Early indications – The concept of the internal market

It is interesting to reflect on the position of the purchaser in the early considerations. David Owen in his book *Our NHS* first published in 1988, ahead of 'Working for Patients', indicated the need for the NHS to move away from a 'broadly collectivist' health service. In a reference to doctors, nurses and producers, he stated that 'in the NHS, they are able to allocate their scarce skills as they feel medical need demands. The problem within the pattern of distributing health care is that it tends to be paternalistic and very unresponsive to patient wishes' (Owen, 1988). He continued by writing that an ideal NHS would be one which balances consumer and producer sovereignty and would never allow either to dominate the other.

'Working for Patients' when published in January 1989 did not give a great deal of guidance on DHA–Trust working together other than through the contract – most evidence coming from the section on Wales and in particular the work of the Welsh Health Planning Forum (Hanson, 1989) which will be referred to below. Even in 'NHS Trusts – A Working Guide' (NHSME, 1990) published in September 1990, the purchaser receives little mention:

> *'Trusts relate to GPs and health authority mainly through the contracts they make with them for the provision of services. Trusts need to work closely with GPs, health authorities and local authority social service departments to make sure that the services they provide or plan to develop, meet identified needs and are properly integrated with other services'.*

The only surprising element about the ministerial statement in early 1993 to give greater emphasis to the 'Purchasing Element' is its lateness, 'from first to last it is the district's and family health services authorities which should be in control. They pay the piper, they must call the tune' (Mawhinney, 1993). However, I believe this again fails to fully appreciate the need for a balance between the power of the purchasers and the providers.

This lack of perception of the fundamental need of a close and constructive relationship between purchaser and provider contrasts most significantly with any working guide issued by such companies as Marks & Spencer or Peugeot Talbot where constructive if 'persuasive' working with other elements is paramount.

This early emphasis on the role of the trust and indeed concentration on trust activities ran the risk of a slow start by the purchaser which was aided by the insistence of the steady state, at least for the DHA purchaser as opposed to perhaps a GP fundholder purchaser. As is to be expected, a number of purchasers made significant early progress where the new role was more easily appreciated and where delegation and devolution to units was already a reality. (To quote the Hanson Profile, 'Our philosophy is to develop, promote and delegate real authority to managers of the highest quality').

The purchaser's role

The perception of the trust by the purchaser is more satisfactory and constructive if the purchaser is clear in its role. I believe that if this is described in simple terms such as to improve the health state and lifestyle of the population for which it has the responsibility achieved through the purchase from trusts and other providers of care which best meets the needs and expectations of those for whom it is purchased.

To be successful in its relationship the purchaser must have established an expertise and confidence in its own responsibility. If its main objectives are as indicated above, it may be able to gain the respect of the provider (and the various customers) and avoid provider dominance. If this can be seen as a significant function which is undertaken with a significant degree of objectivity, expertise and with a clear success criteria, there will be a more constructive relationship.

The provider's role

I believe that the reforms have tended to change certain values although this to an extent at least is subject to geographical and other factors. Whilst the purchaser has, for the first time, perhaps, a clearly defined population for which it has responsibility, the trust, whilst very unwise to neglect its local catchment, is more concerned about its overall business success. This is less so in the case of a community trust. It can be argued that providing that the income is forthcoming, it is not too significant from where it comes. Perhaps it can be compared with the study of the exports of a nation state. A large home market such as enjoyed by the manufacturers in Japan strengthens the opportunity for the export market. This concerns me to some extent as a purchaser, in that it can result in demand not being met for some local needs.

However, the pursuit of 'profitable lines only' has not been realised. There is however a danger of 'cream skimming' – perhaps in a different form to that referred to by Alan Shiell when contrasting self governing trusts with the system in the USA. Whilst price should equal cost and therefore not offer a fundamental risk, there are clearly certain services perhaps because of lack of volume, lack of political or emotional clout which are not as attractive to provide locally and for which local populations are required to make other arrangements.

What the purchaser wants to know about the provider

I believe that it is correct to say that most purchasers do not possess a great deal of market intelligence about various providers. This intelligence should cover the following characteristics of the organisation:

- its philosophy, ability and staff willingness to follow this through;
- its range of products/services;
- quality of products/services;
- price of products services;
- financial viability;
- clinical competence;
- management competence;
- research and development and future plans;
- willingness to work to further develop product range and quality;
- comprehension of the integrated nature of care and a willingness to work with other partners particularly where the trust is not of an integrated nature;
- availability of information;
- willingness to look towards the longer term;
- vision of the future need and delivery of health care.

Working together towards a partnership

In the market intelligence schedule shown above, there are many areas which demand a close working together. I believe there are many people employed in the NHS who would be very surprised by the degree of co-operation which takes place between competitors in the same commercial or industrial activity. Therefore it is perhaps not surprising that at least initially there was an unwillingness to realise how fundamental it is for purchasers and providers to work together in the NHS.

A major task of the purchasers is Health Needs Assessment and, this is illustrated in Figure 6.1 which is taken from the publication of the Information Management Group of the NHSME. This shows the management process relating health needs to heath care contracting. I believe that this requires a great deal of working together between a whole range of providers. It is, I believe, an indictment that too little emphasis is put on this working together with purchasers in many NHS trust applications.

As mentioned before, I believe that the Welsh Health Planning Forum (Hanson, 1989) has led the way with its development of Health Protocols, 'Clinicians of all types, managers, self help and voluntary groups; researchers and individuals are brought together from across Wales to form the Panels of Review – for health gain, people centredness and resource effectiveness; and they are assisted by

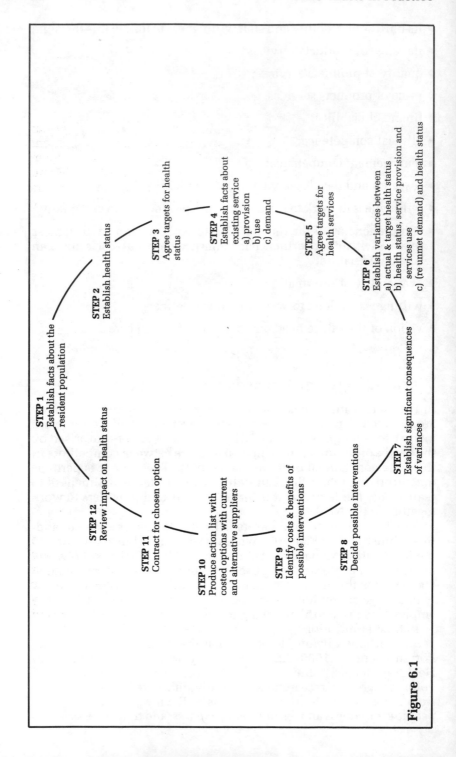

Figure 6.1

internationally recognised appraisers. The Panel members as opinion formers become ambassadors for implementation in their own districts'. Perhaps this is an opportunity of which certain regional health authorities in England are not taking full advantage.

A brief reference to commerce and industry provides numerous examples of purchaser–provider co-operation. From Peugeot Talbot there is the example of the company as purchaser bringing together all its own expertise, the providers of a particular section of the car production activity as well as its own research and development department from both the UK and France to solve a problem encountered by the UK supplier. The result was predictable and almost immediately achieved – with all sides being clear winners and incidentally Peugeot Talbot picking up the cost of 'failure' of a supplier.

Marks & Spencers furnish numerous examples of a purchaser co-operating with providers to produce a new product, often resulting in a very short period of time between the initial concept of a new product to its appearance on the store shelves. Whilst the original concept may have been conceived by the one party, its research and development would be very much a joint effort, reducing time and cost. This co-operation must be achieved by longer term contracts. Again, I refer to a recent comment by a Marks & Spencer executive who stated that many of the company's providers had been working with them for many years and the intention was to maintain this for many years to come. The aims of both the purchaser and the provider are similar and the key must be for the purchaser to ensure that there are incentives in any contract for ever better performance.

This emphasis on working together must be extended to a willingness to have available and be prepared to exchange key information about the contracts. There must be a vision for an information system in the provider trust which at the time that information for trust purposes is accumulated, similar information is available to the purchaser which will not only provide details associated with control in terms of discharges, invoices and quality factors, but will enable the purchaser to use the information to contribute towards the building up of health profiles. There needs to be a very open policy in sharing results of all quality issues including medical audit and health care outcomes as well as the results of any patient attitude survey. A quid pro quo is the early provision of information on any likely change in the priorities of services by purchasers as a result of a reassessment of the population and population needs.

When ways must part

The comments made so far describe a degree of co-operation which should be able to be maintained. However, the considerable financial pressures can cause friction as well as co-operation. A lack of competence may result in a provider which cannot compete or which cannot develop in what and how it provides. In terms of purchasing it is rarely a matter of 'all or nothing'. A marginal change in volume can significantly affect the income and expenditure of the trust and the purchaser must be prepared to use this tool. The greater the number of purchasers the less effective this mechanism is likely to be. This is of interest where we see mergers or affiliations of purchasers and 'multi-funds' of GP fundholders.

Manpower implications

There has been recent debate as to the experience expected of the chief executive of the purchasing authority. Clearly the type of leadership required both for the purchasing authority and indeed the regional health authority has no doubt changed with the latest reforms. However, in managing an organisation, I believe it is advantageous to have ready access to experience in the commercial or industrial activity concerned. This does not mean that the chief executive must have had a career in health, but should be surrounded by a team where there is a collection of experience. It is interesting to read from John Kotter in *The General Managers* (1982) the following:

> 'in addition to sharing a number of personality characteristics, the General Managers also tended to be very similar in terms of certain aspects of business knowledge and business relationships. Specifically, they were all very knowledgeable about the business they were in and they all had an exclusive set of relationships with people throughout their companies and often throughout their industries ... the typical General Manager was an 'expert' in his business. He knew a great deal about the specific products, competitors, markets, customers, techniques, unions and government regulations associated with his industry.'

I have quoted the above in considerable detail because I am concerned at the potential lack of understanding of the business of health because of a lack of staff mobility between purchasers and providers of the various aspects of health care. I believe that it is now somewhat rare for a provider chief executive to prohibit direct contact with say a clinical director by a purchasing organisation, but there remains the need for a flow of professional and managerial staff between the two functions. Both good providers and good purchasers will determine the success of the new concepts and I believe that good purchasers will have an improved opportunity for success if they have had the benefit of experience in the provider units. The opportunity exists for a form of staff rotation. Any unwillingness to share in this prompts the question as to whether both providers and purchasers see themselves as part of one organisation, the NHS.

The future

In examining the purchaser perspective on NHS trusts, I have concentrated on present perspectives. Prior to the introduction of 'Working for Patients' (DH, 1989) and associated reforms, there were enormous differences in the performance and philosophies of the various parts of the NHS jigsaw. The change to a trust model will not immediately transform all providers into a high standard of performance. I believe, however, that it has helped to provide more easily information upon which performance can be judged, needs met and resources obtained.

More detailed opinions are provided elsewhere on the future for the trusts and I am sure that this includes the political implications. I have mentioned above the inevitable coming together of providers once the realities begin to become clearer to trust leaders. Further into the future the possibilities of 'management buyout' opportunities and for different structural relationships with the private sector will develop. This may include direct purchase of the trust by the private sector or entrepreneurs, sections of the trust being franchised or more simply the increase in joint ventures for particular projects. I believe that there will also be opportunities for the larger corporations to develop, whether within or without the NHS resembling a model not dissimilar to say the Henry Ford Health System. As a purchaser, it is important that the system which evolves is one which will lead to a more effective vertical integration of health care services. There must be a greater incentive for care to be provided in the most appropriate setting. The contract is a tool to enable this to take place. There must be more incentives built into the system – not necessarily along the lines of those adopted by the insurance companies in the USA, which are essentially an attempt to curtail expenditure and to influence clinical practices in terms of length of stay and standard procedures. Perhaps it would not be totally inappropriate to remind ourselves of the situation in the USA regarding costs where it has been stated that the problem of escalating costs mainly reflects the fragmentation of purchasing power caused by a myriad of separate private schemes. The article by Michael Prowse writing in the Financial Times (June 20, 1991) stated that costs are restrained by large purchasing organisations.

The NHS has not always been characterised by its ability to change or at least evolve to meet changing circumstances. As a purchaser, I believe that the trust unit has this opportunity through more focused management arrangements of which the Clinical Directorate is of paramount importance. The decision maker is more easily identified. However, what happens is more often the result of an individual or individuals rather than the system. A study of companies or schools is often best undertaken by an examination of the abilities and performance of leaders of such organisations and the health care trust is no exception to this.

References

Department of Health (1989) 'Working for Patients', Cmnd 555, London: HMSO.

Hanson (1989) 'Local Strategies for Health: A New Approach to Strategic Planning – Welsh health Planning Forum', Annual Report of Hanson plc.

Kotter, J. (1982) The General Managers New York: New York Free Press.

Mawhinney, B. (1993) Ministerial Statement, April.

National Health Service Management Executive, (1990) NHS Trusts: A Working Guide, London: HMSO.

Owen, D. (1988) Our NHS London: Pan Books.

Prowse, M. (1991) 'Biting the Bullet on Health Care' Financial Times, 24 June.

Shiell, A. Self Governing Trusts: An Agenda for Evaluation York: University of York.

Purchaser Perspective B

Chris West

When the White Paper 'Working for Patients' was published in January 1989, two innovations attracted attention, GP fundholding and NHS Trusts; each being an important step in unlocking some of the bureaucratic rigidities on the supply side of the NHS. Over the following three years a great deal of effort went into establishing viable trusts, getting the medical profession to accept fundholding and to establish the basic elements of contracting between health authorities and providers. The development of the purchasing function received relatively modest attention, although one project paper, 'Project 26', (1992) did address the development needs of health authorities in their purchasing role.

A major shift in emphasis to purchasing health care, or more appropriately commissioning health care, was heralded by the Secretary of State at her speech to the NAHAT conference on 23 February 1993. The focus of the conference was on the role of the Intermediate Tier and the future of RHAs. But much more significant was the emphasis Virginia Bottomley put on the importance of the purchaser 'being the person who pays the piper and calls the tune'.

In June 1992, the Wessex RHA took the decision to establish six health commissions to bring together the responsibility for purchasing health care across the region. The health commissions are non-statutory bodies which act as the managerial agents of DHAs and FHSAs. In two cases the health commissions are co-terminous with the DHA and FHSA boundaries (the Isle of Wight and Dorset) but in the other four cases (Wiltshire and Bath; Southampton and South West Hants; North and Mid Hants; and Portsmouth and South East Hants), the health commission boundaries are based on those of one or more DHAs.

The model of health commissions, with the responsibility of commissioning care right across the spectrum (primary, community, secondary and tertiary), is a model which has gained a great deal of recognition and support, not just within the Wessex region, but elsewhere in the NHS. Furthermore the Audit Commission, in two reports published in May 1993, (one on the role of DHAs, the other on the role of FHSAs) makes a strong recommendation for primary legislation to be enacted to merge DHAs with FHSAs into unified purchasing organisations.

The advantages of this model are clear. First, an integrated approach to health needs assessment makes a more effective use of the data captured by GPs as well as the data provided by more traditional sources such as health needs assessment surveys, community service information systems, and the data available from the hospital information systems of Providers. Secondly, it provides a much greater opportunity to reinforce the increasing emphasis on primary health care. This is partly as a result of switching DHA funds into primary care. For example, in Portsmouth and South East Hampshire, the Health Commission has used DHA resources to establish a primary care development fund of £500,000 which is being allocated across 14 development programmes. The projects cover a wide range of areas including minor surgery, mental health counselling, practice-based physiotherapy, Community Care management at practice level and pilot projects to capture practice-based morbidity data for Health Needs Assessment. However, the focus on primary care is reinforced by health commissions in other ways as well. In respect of GP fundholding, the legal responsibility for setting the budgets for GP fundholders lies with the Wessex RHA, but the work to set the budget is done within the health commissions. Even in neighbourhoods in which there are no GP fundholders, the development of locality based purchasing as a valid alternative to fundholding enables contracting for secondary care to be done increasingly on a practice centred basis, reinforcing the importance of primary care.

A health commission and any other form of purchasing organisation has a choice and philosophy of the type of style and relationship it wishes to have with its providers. But if the purchaser is to be the person, who not only 'pays the Piper' but effectively 'calls the tune', then this represents a fundamental shift in the balance of power within the National Health Service. A shift in control of even greater distinction and significance than the introduction of general management. Purchasers can choose to either take the initiative gently and with the consent of providers, or they can decide to be more deliberate and assertive. The reforms will only deliver the maximum health care and economical benefits through the latter approach for the following reasons:

- The provider led culture is strong through the National Health Service. It has developed over more than 40 years and if it is to be changed it needs to be confronted assertively.

- Those state corporations which were created after the Second World War and privatised in the 1980s moved rapidly to eliminate wasteful and uneconomic capacity and to significantly reduce manpower. The introduction of an internal market in the National Health Service will lead to similar changes affecting clinical practice, other working practices, the number of employees, and employment terms and conditions of service. These changes represent an enormous challenge to the managers of providers which for quite understandable reasons many of them would prefer not to face.

- The very clear lead given by ministers to give a wider role in the provision of health care to the private sector emphasises the determination of the Government to press forward in an extremely determined manner with the NHS reforms.

So what measures need to be taken by a purchaser in pursuing an assertive approach.

Strategy

It is clearly essential for every purchasing organisation to have a strategy about its priorities and range of services for which it will contract to improve health gain of its local community. Such a strategy has to be based not just on the best evidence or professional advice but also supported in a way that demonstrates the confidence of local citizens and is supported by a range of other organisations – local authorities, voluntary organisations and of course local general practitioners.

Whilst the prime focus for the internal market has been elective surgery in the acute sector – and undoubtably this still remains the major area of potential competition – it would be naive to underestimate the potential for competition in community based health care. GP fundholding and provider based organisations in moving to supply services to the Social Services will undoubtably encroach on territory traditionally covered by community based providers. In particular the voluntary sector as well as independent providers will focus on opportunities for community based services because the relatively low level of capital investment required for market entry and the degree to which much of that capital investment can be put to alternative uses in the event of a business failure will minimise risk. For the acute provider, the expansion of day surgery with a potential for community hospitals to expand into this area, the expansion of increased care in people's homes and the expanded role of the GP and practice-centred primary care all represent a significant threat. Success for either category of NHS provider is measured in one simple way – survival.

As usual, changes to the NHS in London have attracted the most attention particularly following publication of the Tomlinson Report (1992) and the Secretary of State's response to that document. However, in many other parts of the country, purchasers are beginning to stimulate the market. In Southampton and South West Hampshire and Portsmouth and South East Hampshire, the two health commissions which cover southern Hampshire are working purposely together to ensure there is effective competition between the acute based providers. These are the Southampton University Hospitals, the Royal Hampshire County Hospital in Winchester, St Mary's Hospital in the Isle of Wight, St Richard's Hospital in Chichester, the Royal Bournemouth Hospital, Portsmouth Hospitals, the Royal Naval Hospital at Haslar and of course the private sector.

The reason for this approach is because of the belief that it is only through the purchaser taking a firm lead and deliberately extending competition between providers that the Trusts will focus their business on the purchasers agenda, aim to improve quality, drive down costs through the elimination of waste and change clinical practice in line with the best in the country. Each of the two commissions is prepared to work with providers to achieve efficiency of savings by sharing comparative information and to support providers through the inevitable process of down-sizing capacity which may in the short term lead to an increase in fixed costs. It is clearly beneficial to providers and purchasers to have a long term relationship based on agreed patterns of investment particularly where a provider needs to make major capital investment in order to supply services against a purchasing authority's long term purchasing strategy. Commissions can also help in two other areas in order to create a more predictable environment for providers. The first is to make sense of the wider agenda emerging through 'Health of the Nation' (1991) with local authorities and voluntary organisations. All trusts need to have a strong external focus, but given the pressure on them to improve service quality and reduce costs, it is inevitable that provider managers will have a strong internal focus in the short to medium term. Therefore the opportunity to have purchasers analysing and interpreting external trends is a significant opportunity. The second way in which Purchasers might help providers is in their relationship with GP fundholders. This assistance can be done by providing a strategic framework focused on health gain for each of the two parties.

However, two factors frequently impede the development of mature relationships between purchasers and providers. The first is the lack of the strategic framework provided to the purchaser, the second is a 'victim mentality' that many providers have acquired since becoming independent of their parent body. Providers have to understand that purchasers may not be interested in either what the provider has provided in the past or what it now wants to provide. What matters is what the customer wants and, it is only through providing the services that the customer wants, that providers earn the right to stay in business. There is still too much of the mentality which can easiest be described as that prevailing in British Leyland in the 1970s as opposed to that manifest by the Nissan car plant in County Durham in the 1990s.

Purchasers will want providers to contribute to their agenda but in order to gain entry to do so, the relationship between the two bodies has to be honest and straightforward with a disinterest in trivia. The provider needs to continually demonstrate that it is a reliable organisation and that what is promised up front in the negotiations with the purchaser is deliverable through internal control mechanisms. In this way, each can regard the other as a reliable partner to the relationship.

In peeling back the traditional introspection in both management and values that prevails in many parts of the Health Service, there are a number of measures that can be taken. First, the purchaser can make available simple information about Charter standards and outpatient waiting times to all GPs in the area covered by a commission. This information should include outpatient information not just for the providers based within the area covered by the commission but those bordering as well. The aim must be to stimulate GP's to think 'market'. Secondly, it is important to bond together primary and secondary care through developing initiatives which enhance communication between GPs and consultant staff, for example the development of referral guidelines and protocols. The latter are particularly valuable in providing a basis for good quality care, development of audit and educational programmes to underpin and improve the practice of health care. Thirdly, the provision of more explicit information to the public.

For some time many health authorities have undertaken surveys of both consumer views and health and lifestyle surveys but what is a much greater challenge is in gauging the views of the 'healthy public' in the debate about location type, style and priorities for health services. To undertake this task in Portsmouth and South East Hampshire there are not only a series of consumer involvement groups and consumer panels based in different localities throughout the district but also the health commission run adult education classes so that the level of understanding and awareness increasingly spreads throughout the community. Change can also be promoted in other quite simple ways. For example in the area covered by the commission we have one Patient's Charter covering all health service facilities and a joint leaflet between Health and Social Services on how to make suggestions and complaints. Nothing can be worse for the confused and uncertain citizen than to be faced with a plethora of Charters and complaints procedures and to find that it is only at the sixth attempt that the right procedure is being used. Again, in Portsmouth, to help provide information to the public the document 'Healthwise', an A to Z of all local Health Services, has been published. The initial print of 10,000 copies was rapidly consumed – one major local employer asked immediately for 200 copies to distribute throughout his organisation.

So what goals should a purchaser be aiming for? The first is to recognise the purchaser's key responsibility for setting the agenda for health gain and being relatively unconcerned for the organisational implications for established providers of any adverse consequences which flow from the fulfilment of the purchaser's goals. Second, to create openness within and about the local health services – their costs, quality, and performance – and to seek and publish consumer views on these services. Third, where either efficiency or customer acceptability are enhanced, then with support from GPs to shift service provision to a primary care from a secondary care setting. Fourth, to stimulate an understanding within local communities and local organisations, both statutory and non-statutory, in local health services so that local citizens have the knowledge and information to contribute to the debate about health priorities. Provision of information to both GPs and local citizens is the most important ingredient for success. Information must be made available to the public and to GPs about a range of matters which hitherto professional staff, and many managers, have wished to neither disclose or to discuss. Without a doubt, the emphasis and initiative in the NHS have shifted to the purchasers – they must now get on and deliver.

References

Audit Commission, (1993) *Their Health, Your Business*, London: HMSO

Audit Commission, (1993) *Practices Make Perfect*, London: HMSO.

Department of Health, (1989) 'Working for Patients', Cmnd 555, London: HMSO.

Department of Health, (1991) 'Health of the Nation', Cmnd 1523, London: HMSO.

National Health Services Management Executive, (1992) *Local Voices*, London.

7 NHS trusts – two provider perspectives: views from the bridge

Judy Hargadon

Provider perspective A

Why become a trust?

To understand the impact of trust status on provider units and how that change in status has affected the delivery of service and style of management, it is important to understand where the first wave applicants were coming from and why they chose to apply for trust status.

Most first wave trusts were well advanced managerially and in terms of service delivery. In the case of Croydon community services, we saw ourselves as amongst the leaders of units delivering community-based care. We were one of the first community units to set up neighbourhood services, a concept promoted in the NHS in general by the Cumberledge report (1986). Staff were organised to enhance close working with GPs, a scheme generally known as 'GP attachment'. We had introduced care group planning mechanisms that involved the public as well as staff and managers in developing plans for future services. We were developing multi-disciplinary protocols for patient treatments and improving information to the public, devolving managerial responsibility for budgets and encouraging staff to take cost into account in decisions about patterns of care. Our integrated planning and review process was linked to personal appraisal. In our own assessment we were relatively well-advanced in our thinking and in our managerial practice, and therefore well-placed to take on the demands of self management. Most other first wave applicants felt the same.

In addition to its own sense of confidence, however, each of the first wave trusts had other reasons for applying as well; for example;

the desire to be free from insensitive management at 'higher' levels of the NHS; the desire to be seen as a progressive provider of care; the wish to get recognition for the good work it already was doing; or even the concern about what might happen to the unit or to people's jobs if the unit did not become a trust. There was also a genuine belief amongst many in the new purchaser–provider model being introduced to the NHS and a political or practical desire to make it work.

We applied for Trust status for two inter-related reasons, the wish to be in the forefront of change and the need to strengthen community care.

To be successful, organisations need to scan the environment for change and decide how to respond. Whilst we did not spend a lot of time discussing whether trusts were a good thing in themselves, the question we did debate fully and openly was, 'If trusts are going to be introduced to the NHS, would it be a good idea to be involved in this move at the beginning?' Our answer was, of course, 'yes'. We believed that if a change was coming it was much better to be in the forefront where you could help shape the way in which that change was implemented and where developmental support would be greatest. Secondly, given that we recognised an increased power to negotiate with purchasers as a great advantage of trust status, we did not believe it would be good for community care if only hospitals got trust status in the first wave. We thought with only hospitals working as independent providers, the 'dumping' problems that many community units experience could increase, with community nurses expected to pick up even more workload discharged from trust hospitals with no increase in resourcing. In our view, it was important to have community units in amongst provider trusts right from the beginning to keep a negotiated balance in NHS care.

As a unit we have developed in many ways and have no regrets about becoming a trust. There are serious concerns for the NHS to consider about the fact that the potential the system offered has not been realised. Indeed, as we consider the strengths and weaknesses of trusts as a mechanism for service delivery we have to remember that the system was piloted on units with strong managerial support. As it is extended to all units, the NHS must ask whether they will all be strong enough managerially to handle the added responsibilities and realise their full potential within the system as it works. Later in the chapter I will explain and analyse these concerns more fully and make suggestions about how to move forward.

Developing into trusts

Most trusts have grown in their capacity to deliver good services effectively, as material circulated by the Management Executive has shown. This development has come as much from the process of setting up as a trust as from actually running as a trust. The selection process for first wave trusts was very rigorous and set many demands. The learning curve was steep. In our case we have noticed the following areas of development.

Systems sensitive to service delivery

We now have much better financial information than in the past and a support system that is designed for community services not institutions.

We have got rid of rigid procedures, particularly in the field of nursing and supplies, which were made by large bureaucratic organisations that were frightened of devolving responsibilities to staff because they felt distant from them.

We are now able to negotiate terms and conditions of employment directly with our staff. Employees in community services have been as ill-served by the staff side of Whitley, as have managers of units like ours by the management side, when it comes to terms and conditions that suit community services. We can, and have, negotiated small things which help both parties and are cost-effective, in a climate that is challenging to both parties but not provocative, mistrusting and time-wasting as has been the case with national negotiations, for example, carer leave, which is very important to the kind of staff we employ, in return for more flexibility, which is important for our varying workloads; flexible incremental payments to encourage training and good development in the job, which is good for mature applicants who learn quickly.

Clarity about service expectations

We have become much more explicit about what we can and cannot do with the resources that the district health authority is willing to put into our services as a result of the contracting process. Although a hospital ward will experience different workloads according to the nature of the patients they are looking after, at least the fixed number of beds gives a limit to the amount of work it is assumed the nursing staff and the hospital will take on at any time. In the past, there was no such controlling measure to keep workloads safe in the community. Contracting helps to develop clearer expectations about workloads that will maintain safety and quality, and forces choices upon purchasers and providers about where to put resources to ensure this.

This better clarity about what can and cannot be provided is important for the public who have in the past expected the NHS to provide services beyond the means available. Better information to the public is also in line with the Patients' Charter.

Improved Management

Trust boards are interested in management of the organisation, not in looking impressive in public meetings as was so often the case with health authority meetings in the past. The non-executive Board members try to help the executives maintain an overview of the organisation, again unlike the past when the monthly health authority meeting often saw members criticising the executives for the effects of implementing policies that those very members had discussed and agreed at previous meetings. This change has been enormously important to the confidence of NHS managers, a group that have not always been well supported by their political masters. This confidence shows itself in improved management and hence improved delivery of service.

Trust status has brought nearer to individual managers the responsibility they hold for the good use of resources as there is no-one else to blame now when things go wrong.

Development of staff

There is a much greater awareness amongst the staff that the NHS is a political instrument as well as an organisation delivering health care, and as a result staff are better able to understand, and hence influence, how decisions about funding and direction are made. The clearer management lines have made it possible to improve information to staff generally.

The transition to trust status proved to the staff that they have the skills needed to cope with, and to gain from change. This helped them to prepare for an even bigger change, the ability of GP fundholders to purchase our community services. The pace of change in their working lives and the delivery of health care has been hard for many NHS employees to accept. There is considerable resistance to change throughout the NHS, but we have found it to be much less the case as a result of our successful change to trust status.

Streamlined management

Above all we have learnt that it is possible for small organisations to develop ways of working that are cost-effective and that also ensure that you have the right expertise when you need it. You do not need large separate specialist management departments to execute many tasks. You do need expert advice and the ability to recognise when and how to get it. It is possible to 'buy in' small bits of specific expertise whilst developing a much better understanding of an issue within a small general management team. For example, we have found that we do not need a vast works department to plan and manage estate developments. We manage the scheme ourselves and buy in expert architectural, engineering, and other advice as needed.

It takes no more time than it used to take chasing the works department to find out whether the work was being done. We've learnt the hard way sometimes but have achieved things faster than when we were dependent on large hierarchical departments to achieve them for us.

We can set priorities for these tasks in a way that suits the needs of our organisation, not those of functional departments with agendas of their own. Let me be clear, I'm not arguing against the need for expert departments and individuals when it makes managerial sense to distribute staffing resources in this manner. However, in so many parts of the NHS functional management departments like personnel, planning, information, estates and finance have developed ways of working which complicate and delay rather then enable the effective delivery of services.

Best of all has been the opportunity to handle our own planning applications. This has been an extremely difficult and sometimes painful process but we have been able to challenge those against us with a passion and package of information about the service which distant planners and works staff never had. Less and less do we find ourselves saying 'what a pity we couldn't . . .' Less and less do we experience the frustration of wishing 'they' had said certain things to push our case.

The sense of control over some small, some large, but all significant matters, has given trusts a new enthusiasm, a belief that improvements for patients can be made that before were not felt to be possible. Trust status and the work involved in getting there have clearly given benefits to the NHS, whilst being very demanding for the staff involved. These benefits will be lost and the effort wasted if we do not make sure that the contracting system with independent providers continues to develop.

The future growth of trusts

We have not yet realised the full potential of a system of independently run organisations getting work on their ability to deliver for purchasers who are focusing on the needs of their population. To do this the NHS must tackle two issues; the failure to give the internal market a chance to work because of the constant application of political override, and the inadequate development of purchasing, both of which mean that staff in trusts are working harder than before just to stand still.

As the Americans have found, a system left to the market does not automatically achieve political goals. Even attempts to ensure immunisation by the States, who in some cases paid the full costs of the drugs, failed to achieve reasonable coverage in some areas because the system of delivery was unacceptable to many parents. If governments want a market in health care, even a well regulated internal market, they have to be prepared to allow some places to do better than others. This is politically risky, but 'bailing out' those who cause political storms by failing, for example, those with long waiting lists, creates a disincentive to the efficient practice that competition encourages. If these risks are unacceptable, it is wasteful to set up a machinery to enable competition. Assuming that some form of internal market is to continue, we must rely more confidently on the ways it works for improvements, and not too easily suspend or interfere with it.

Few first wave trusts have easy and effective working relationships with their purchasers. This is for a number of reasons:

- As the reforms were introduced, trusts were developed first and were given a very high profile. Many district officers had seen their previous role as one of managing multiple provider units and resented the loss of direct managerial control of those units. Indeed many chose to become trust chief executives, often trying to take whole districts into trust status. This was not helpful to the self esteem of those in purchasing.

- Not being used to a market, and indeed, often having joined the NHS because we did not like the notion of operating within a market, many managers have neither the skills, inclination, understanding, or experience of the kind of negotiation which makes a market culture work properly.

- Neither party in the contracting relationship seems to understand where it has power and control and where the boundaries of these lie. There are examples of trusts refusing to give information to purchasers in response to perfectly legitimate requests to do so. Likewise some purchasers use contracts to try to instruct units in micro detail how to deliver services. You often hear the complaint, from both sides, that the other party has all the power, which has led to petty and futile attempts to redress the perceived imbalance.

- Most purchasers also have had directly-managed units to run, which takes time away from purchasing, whether regretted or not, and can lead to favouritism towards the DMU in contracting, whether intended or not.

- Many districts have excluded providers from planning because they believe that providers, especially trusts, will try to skew the planning to make more business for themselves.

If we are to continue with trusts we have to find some new ways forward. Its easy to look back and comment on what we should have done. For example, the contracting relationship has become most sophisticated in districts where all provider units became trusts at the same time. A concentration of effort on a few real working models might have been a better approach then the scattered first wave. However none of this is to be. At this stage, effective ways of making progress need to be found before we reach a stage, not unlike those reforming the health care in the United States have to face, where everyone blames everyone else for the problems and increased costs, leaving members of the public as pawns in a complex muddle.

To do this there first needs to be joint training for both parties, to develop the working relationships required for effective negotiation, specification, implementation and evaluation of contracts which produce good quality, targeted services and value for money. Discussion with those in other organisations with similar roles would help this development. Developing the behaviours required and then leaving people to develop systems locally will have a much greater impact than sending out instructions from the centre on how to do it.

Secondly, planning should be separated from contracting. When planning for a future service, current and potential providers should be involved fully in discussing the shape of the future service, the likely costs and feasibility of implementation. Providers can bring a very realistic set of information to the planning table. If the process is based on evidence and involves enough potential competitors, ie at least two, 'business seeking' should not be a problem. Once the service direction and shape is determined, the purchasers can then set a contract specification in line with their overall plans for services and providers can be invited to tender for the contract, either individually or jointly. Having involved the providers in the planning in an open fashion, the proposals submitted are more likely to meet the purchasers' aspirations and there will be a sense amongst providers that they were given a fair chance to bid for the work.

Thirdly, ways must be found to improve purchaser performance. In true markets like those in the USA there is genuine competition between purchasers because people can change their health plans, ie their purchases, every year and employers can cease to contract with an insurance company if it is not purchasing the kind of care, at an acceptable price, required for its employees. There is therefore a great incentive to purchase effectively.

There is no such incentive in our system because the public do not have the discretion to change to another purchaser if they do not like what the district health authority serving them is buying. Through the introduction of contracting and competition, we have brought into the NHS market incentives for efficiency and effectiveness on the providing side, but not so on the purchasing side. Regions now have some bureaucratic powers to correct poor purchasing, but these do not appear to be sufficient. This needs to be re-addressed.

Fourthly, and leading on from this, we have failed to recognise how much regulation is needed in a market where consumers are vulnerable. In the USA, where a market in health care operates fully, if not perfectly, there are many regulations covering delivery of health care and extensive external accreditation mechanisms which are taken very seriously. The NHS does not need pages and pages of rules, but it does need mechanisms which enable the contracting system to work effectively in the interests of patients. We do not yet have an effective form of regulation. Regions have been given a role in the arbitration and conciliation process, but as trusts are monitored by outposts who report to a different division of the management executive than regions there have been problems regulating the market. The organisational point at which disputes between purchasers and providers ultimately meet is on Duncan Nichol's desk. This cannot be efficient or effective. In addition, the obsession of some trusts to be free of regional interference, and the determination of some regions to interfere inappropriately in local contracting matters, led to indecision at the centre about revised arrangements for the intermediate tier in the NHS. This delay has been very damaging to the development of a proper internal market and has led to a continuation of the old behaviours of pleasing the next level up the system to get projects through the system, rather than to development of market-style thinking. In fact this activity requires more time than in the past because one now has to 'please' the outposts as well as the district, region, and Department of Health, let alone all local interests. As all the 'fresh blood' brought into the new NHS in the form of non-executive directors get used to this style of working, we will lose the advantage of their new way of thinking in implementing the market approach.

Lastly it is important to recognise the need to learn as we go and not to give up. The NHS has not gained as many benefits in terms of increased efficiency as expected from trust status. Partly the system has caused this as outlined above but trusts must also share the responsibilty. Some trusts have refused to give relevant information to purchasers which then affects their attitude to all trusts. Some trusts have continued to operate as if they were still directly managed units leaving the purchaser with old as well as new responsibilities. As a trust, it can be hard to know where the right balance lies. For example, when trying to raise prices to cover new costs, how much detail should be given to purchasers to explain the calculation and confirm that one is pricing at cost as the regulations require. Too little explanation makes the purchaser suspicious and leaves the trust open to allegations of mismanagement. Too full an explanation encourages the purchaser to get involved in the minutiae of running the trust.

There are many lessons that we can learn from practice over time, if we work within a climate that recognises the unique roles and responsibilities of all those involved in the internal health care market. We can not learn if we are constantly drawn back into a centrally controlled and dominated system. If the latter is what our political leaders want, then I suggest they need to reconsider the very idea of a market in health care in the first place.

Provider perspective B

Mike Fry

In my two year experience as a chief executive I have found a widespread tendency to greatly over-simplify trust status. This has led to the most casual of observers swiftly adopting a stance regarding NHS trusts, often based on the most flimsy acquaintance with the powers of trusts or indeed with any facts concerning them. For me, the reality of 'self government' has been a complex blend of liberation, frustration, enervation and a heightened sense of both organisational potential and personal achievement.

I have no doubts that trust status has very positively aided the development of Christie Hospital; however I can be equally confident that few first wave chief executives could be as unequivocally positive as myself. Much of this relates to our former position as one of four units within a very large, financially straitened, teaching health authority. The Christie is a specialist cancer centre with substantial associated research and other specialist facilities – almost entirely non-exchequer funded – and as such was always a cuckoo in a health authority nest. Attempts at becoming the first non-London special health authority had failed in the past and consequently the prospect of self governing status was immediately attractive to a number of key opinion formers on the site. This is not to play down both the internal and the considerable external opposition to the Christie trust application but rather to indicate at the outset that the organisation had an instinctively more positive reaction to the allure of trust status than was the case in many other places.

A related point was the fact that clinicians within the Christie Hospital, in common with many hospitals, had been seeing an ever rising number of patients against a backdrop of modest – at best – increases in funding. The prospect of 'money following patients' was an immediate and very important selling point to clinicians for the reforms. How this principle could apply within a cash limited health system was never adequately addressed in the immediate aftermath of the White Paper launch and as the reforms were subjected to greater scrutiny the 'money following patients' catchphrase of the politicians was dropped. Nonetheless this tenet of the White Paper remains fixed in the minds of many busy doctors. It helped to keep the reforms afloat during an especially turbulent period but is now a cause of much medical cynicism in these still largely block contract days.

Impact of managerial culture

To have any understanding of the changes to management culture one needs an insight into the trust application process. This entailed managers, many of whom were unit general managers taking centre stage in a public and political battle the ferocity of which the NHS had not previously seen. Managers were not only expected to lead their organisations but also to promote a key feature of a radical set of government reforms. The net result was an initial group of trust chief executives who were chastened by the hostility encountered during the trust consultation period but who significantly grew in confidence as a result of seeing through an especially difficult task.

The trust concept was controversial and the road to it strewn with obstacles of varying size, not least the boulder concerning one's personal position. From an early stage it was made clear to first wave 'sponsors' that they should not see themselves as automatically becoming chief executives. Dark rumours circulated regarding the openness of competition for chief executive posts and of the likely preferences of Shadow Trust Chairmen – the majority of whom emerged only in the Autumn of 1990. Such a set of circumstances is hardly what the organisational change textbooks recommend but perhaps seeing through a project in this way served to heighten the personal satisfaction at the end of it. Certainly for me whilst battling so long and hard to keep the application viable I had developed a deep commitment for the embryonic trust and an intense belief in what it could achieve. To be given the opportunity to help fulfil this potential by becoming chief executive genuinely did ultimately feel like a privilege . . . albeit one I had worked hard to get. There was also a hefty challenge to one's personal pride in realising the self governing goal. There were few senior health service staff who previously did not regularly indulge in protracted grumbling about the procrastination, poor judgement or incompetence of the district or regional tiers. In the early days of trust expressions of interest the notion of self government seemed frankly unrealistic and hopelessly unachievable but over time it largely became a reality. (Though it would be dishonest not to admit to being somewhat daunted by the prospect at times during the transition period).

I also gained enormous satisfaction and confidence from fashioning the trust from very flimsy foundations. For example previously we had a minimal finance presence on the site and effectively no personnel department. Two years later I can point to considerable financial expertise and effective personnel support but without the flabbiness and lack of urgency which had so frustrated myself and colleagues when these weaknesses were encountered in their district equivalents.

Finally, and at the risk of sounding cliched or jingoistic, the first wave chief executives were buoyed by having successfully achieved a major organisational change. That is not to imply unquestioning support for the reforms, even for the concept of trusts, but as managers we had actively led our units towards what we judged was the most advantageous position. During the consultation period we had all too painfully been made aware of the highly charged and party political nature of the changes but these considerations alone were not sufficient to lead us to abandon the project. In short, by successfully concluding a very difficult task we demonstrated to ourselves and our organisations that the trust concept was viable and to be preferred.

Several times in the aforegoing paragraphs I have mentioned confidence in the context of health service managers either having or lacking it. Confidence was also a crucially important factor in the micro-politics of the emergence of trusts. Unit general managers had to tangle with their district general managers and often district chairman at some stage in the development of their bid. Equally the whole district trust sponsors had to face the suspicion, unease and often the opposition of many erstwhile colleagues.

It is easy to forget how riven were all parts of the health service by the reforms when they were first floated. Within most professional groups this led to hostility being directed towards those insiders who were cast as standard bearers for a very threatening series of changes. Hence first wave trusts not only faced flak from outside interests but also from their peers who were opposed to the concept of self governing units.

A second additional source of tension – and ultimately increased confidence – for aspiring trust chief executives, was the way in which the traditional managerial career ladder was challenged. Indeed in many cases the established order became inverted as unit-based posts appeared to offer long term career prospects. Couple this with the uncertainty offered by the purchaser role and the resentment towards 'upstart' UGM's busily preparing trust applications of many old school DGMs may better be understood.

Prior to the White Paper whilst I recognised that visibility and leadership were important features of the general manager's job I would probably have ranked them alongside more traditional skills such as attention to detail or problem solving. I now recognise the very different role of a chief executive which must genuinely encompass the more nebulous notions of leadership and vision. Allied to this is the need for an organisational figurehead, the extent of which will depend upon the attitude and attributes of the trust chairman. All of which is substantially bolstered by managerial confidence, a commitment to the organisation and a belief in its ability to deliver strong performance.

Impact on managerial/medical relationships

This is another area where it is difficult, and probably dangerous, to generalise. At the risk of stating the obvious, the state of medical/ managerial relationships within a trust will depend heavily on the previous state of play and also on the extent to which medical staff supported the application. In more practical terms the method of appointment and ultimately the appointee to the medical director post was crucial to later medical/managerial relations in hospital based trusts.

The trust model offers a much greater opportunity for doctors and managers within an organisation to share a vision. In addition the simple fact that most trusts are of more manageable – in the sense of size – proportions inevitably results in a greater likelihood of doctors and managers feeling a greater shared purpose and organisational loyalty. A further vital, if generally overlooked point is that trust chief executives will almost certainly remain in post longer than their general manager predecessors. It has been common in medical circles for complaints to be voiced that just as a mutual understanding had begun to emerge, able and ambitious general managers were obliged by the career treadmill to depart for pastures new. This has resulted in an understandable cynicism on the part of hospital doctors who expect to complete their career within the same organisation to which they were appointed 30 years previously. Whilst it is unlikely that many chief executives are looking to similarly long periods of tenure a breach of the 'two to three years then move on' principle will enable managers to claim a more legitimate long term interest in the organisation.

When compared with the position of the unit general manager, the chief executive finds him or herself in a much more equal position when dealing with medical staff. Before the reforms there always lurked the possibility of the district general manager or other district powers failing to support the unit management team especially in difficult medical matters. Similarly there was often the difficulty of engaging district minds regarding operational or other issues which might be construed as of minor importance. Conversely, the district tier in most cases was felt to be too remote to actively tackle difficult issues concerning medical personality problems or other equally tricky issues. Whilst easy to dismiss, such matters can make or break a manager's credibility and are also the stuff of which organisational success or failure is made. The trust model has ensured that the boss – be it chairman or chief executive – works within the same building and, hopefully, is also seen on the same corridors.

I have been surprised by the extent to which a greater number of medical staff have genuinely become involved in decision making since the advent of the trust. These doctors may be divided into two groups. A small number understood the old system and concentrated their decision making energies and lobbying where it mattered, at district and health authority level. These 'heavy weights' now operate at trust level.

The second group of doctors are those who previously did not trouble themselves with involvement in the decision making process. This might have been as a result of being disillusioned by the difficulties of 'getting anything done', a disinclination to spend too much time on administrative matters or simply not being fully able to comprehend the committee structures and related forums in which health authority decision making was practised.

From the outset, the Christie Hospital Trust Board made explicit a medical advisory structure. During the first year of operation it became clear that decision making would take place in the appointed forum and on the basis of advice given. Those who had taken part in the process were rewarded – either literally or through having witnessed and participated in the setting of priorities. In this way not only were the initial medical enthusiasts satisfied but others who had remained on the sidelines were encouraged to join the debates over the short and long term future of the organisation.

Furthermore in the course of these debates I was genuinely surprised at the insight and wisdom which medical staff were able to bring to problems which I had previously assumed were mine alone. These ranged from the utilisation of capital stock to the appearance of public areas and from paramedical skill mix to performance related pay. It was not that medical staff had previously not been interested or able to constructively contribute to such matters but rather that the organisational hierarchy and decision making structures did not engage them. (An identical release of energy and wisdom has been witnessed with other groups). In essence the arrogance of the managerial classes was previously compounded by the insensitivity and inappropriateness of the structure.

In summary, whilst the pattern of medical/managerial relationships will never be open to simple explanation, if decision making is genuinely taken at a level closer to where medical practice is undertaken doctors will be more ready and able to participate.

Relationship with purchasers and other bodies

Many commentators of the reforms have fallen into the trap of trying to understand the purchaser–provider relationship from a quasi scientific viewpoint. Organisational motives have been intensely scrutinised, elaborate health needs assessment exercises planned and contract adherence brought centre stage. In reality I have found that individual attitudes and relationships are the most critical factor in determining the nature of the purchaser–provider link. Perhaps this will always be the case but for the early years in particular previous contact between individuals will critically influence working arrangements.

It must be remembered that at a senior level in the NHS the reforms have been accompanied by an unprecedentedly low level of individual geographical movement during a major reorganisation. Hence whilst a fence has been erected, those on either side still remember working together in the recent past. This can make for wholly amicable – at times cosy – working. Alternatively purchasing based on a crude form of revenge may be perpetrated either by former district officers against recalcitrant former units or by macho-trust personnel intent on showing 'who's boss'.

The Christie Hospital trust has an unusually diverse pattern of purchasers. No purchaser alone accounts for more than six and a half per cent of patient activity and we have 26 purchasers who each account for more than one per cent of patient activity. Consequently we have gained a great deal of experience in a short period of how purchasers are approaching their task.

We have found purchasers to be inherently cautious and, to our frustration, consistently reluctant to agree non-block contract terms. They point to the ever-increasing patient referrals, the soaring cost of anti-cancer drugs, the fact that all Christie work is malignancy related and veer away from proposals for more activity-sensitive contracts. This unwillingness to share risk has done much to inhibit development of the purchaser/provider relationship.

Nonetheless, a number of purchasers have approached us in a positive manner, keen to understand the services we provide but honest about their ability to keep pace with medical innovation and activity. In these instances a productive relationship has begun to be forged based on a better understanding of each party's constraints and agenda.

On the negative side I would highlight two failings which have been encountered on a number of occasions. The first concerns the purchasing authority which has become so consumed by considerations of strategy and epidemiology that they struggle to consider any period closer than five years away. This leads to frustration on the part of the provider to engage the other party in current and short term issues but also tends to result in the existing pattern of services being continued. The second unfortunate tendency is for purchasers to prepare complex and mechanistic quality monitoring systems. With few exceptions we have found these to be hopelessly over ambitious, impractical, incapable of enforcing sanctions but most seriously deleterious to the relationship with the provider.

Our view is that service standards are a provider issue and that purchasers can only expect to monitor at arms' length and by exception. Clearly if standards are consistently or dangerously unacceptable then the provider forfeits the right to non-interference in its operations – or alternatively to treat patients from that authority.

Unlike many Trusts the Christie Hospital is principally a tertiary referral centre and therefore we have had only limited involvement with GP fundholders. Of those fund holding practices with which we have come into contact relations have remained cordial and there has been less explicit or implied criticism than has been the case with health authority purchasers.

As a recipient and a provider of support services we have been able to maintain good relationships with adjoining provider units. In the early days of the trust concept some staff within other providers were suspicious or a little hostile towards the embryonic Christie Trust but the previous co-operation was quickly re-established. As most providers are now either operating as trusts or are pursuing an application the supportive nature of inter-provider relations continues. Clearly there may be tensions over specific issues or in regard to overlapping referral territories but my impression is that these are now accepted as intrinsic to the game according to the new rules and outside the underlying spirit of co-operation between health service providers.

In some quarters it has been fashionable to criticise the regional involvement in establishing trusts but I would have to acknowledge considerable help and support during the trust application process from the regional health authority. In our case both the personal and organisational support was invaluable. Notwithstanding this, and in true cocky adolescent style, the Christie Trust is now keen to loosen the apron strings but I am confident that in due course a mature relationship based upon mutual respect will emerge. From the trust perspective I hope this will be with a much slimmed down regional tier primarily concerned with helping services to develop in a sensible and strategically coherent manner.

Relations with local newspapers and the local community health council were very adversely affected during the Christie trust application process. The former are now well on the way to recovery – partly as a result of the lowered national profile of the health service reforms – but the latter relationship has only achieved a state of frosty congeniality.

The principle lesson we learned on the media relations front was that it is not possible to swim against a national tide. During 1990 the national news media gave a strong lead on the NHS reforms and cast the Shadow Trusts as flagships of an undesirable fleet of changes to a much loved national institution. Looking back I now accept that too much energy was spent in attempting to persuade local newspapers of the merits of the trust application. Now that the storm has passed we again enjoy perfectly amicable links with the many local media outlets.

I fear that the problems concerning the relationship between the trust and local community health council is more intractable. It hinges upon the unstated but nonetheless very real dilution of CHC powers brought about by the reforms. Despite this I believe that CHC's could still perform a very valuable role in articulating patients views and acting as proxy 'patients friend' to purchasing authorities. However this relies upon CHC's genuinely embracing the more strategic role inherent to purchasing and in being prepared to distance themselves from the allure of matters operational.

I imagine that my enthusiasm for the Trust model will have been apparent within the first few paragraphs of this section. I hope that by now I will have been able to demonstrate that this enthusiasm has been generated by a realisation of the advantages of trust status rather than simply the position of the writer. Before concluding however I would make mention of four specific areas where important benefits have been realised as a direct result of the Christie Hospital achieving trust status.

Capital improvements

Probably the biggest area of benefit has been with regard to capital improvements. Previously the Christie Hospital was discriminated against by the district health authority because of substantial charitable support. This discrimination no longer applies and the site gets a fair slice of the available capital cake. The benefits also extend to the internal scrutiny which is now applied to capital schemes. In the past the process all too easily resembled a raffle. As the ultimate decision would be taken remote from the unit a number of bids, often without priority, would be submitted and the unit would await the winning ticket. Now under the trust the available expenditure is known and less deserving schemes are challenged and do not make it to the shortlist. Finally, and as part of this process of challenging capital bids, much better use of space has been achieved. Essentially, if there is limited capital available and the same improvement can be achieved by doing away with a staff coffee room or underused office then this course of action is pursued. Yes, such a course of action was possible prior to becoming a trust but for a variety of reasons the most difficult decisions were not taken.

Employment policy

The Christie Trust stated one of its objectives as being to be regarded as a good employer. As we moved into the second year of trust status the executive directors debated how this was best achieved and concluded that this should also mean tackling under performers as well as rewarding good performers. The difficult task of addressing under performance, especially in middle and senior staff, can be tackled in a much more straightforward way in a trust. This has certainly been our experience and the net result is lower management costs, a more effective group of managers but also one where pruning has been achieved in a more dignified manner than was normally the case in the few health authorities where this difficult issue was seriously tackled.

Sacred cows

The third area is the trust's much greater ability to tackle sacred cows. In a hospital setting these can range from status linked dining facilities or car parking places to theatre or outpatient session scheduling or professional skill mix. The ability of professionals –

and within this I would include managers – to obfuscate or to avoid facing up to major issues is much more difficult where decision making is closer to the front line.

Overhead costs

The final major area of benefit which I would draw attention to has been the trust's ability to very substantially reduce its overhead costs. Partly as a result of established organisations tending to become flabby and partly as a result of the trust's commitment to challenging the costs associated with the former regime, we were able to liberate large sums of money which were previously tied up in functions based in the health authority headquarters. I do not think that this was particularly the result of a proliferating district but rather the inherent weakness of a multi-tiered organisation. The hungrier, leaner trust has shown that it can operate at least as well, often better, but with lower overhead costs.

On the debit side my major regret is that we have not been able to exploit the many opportunities for introducing greater flexibility in staff terms and conditions and also in staffing arrangements. Initially this process was inhibited by the conspiracy theories perpetuated by many of the staff organisations but more recently progress could have been made. Sadly I fear that we are not alone in having failed to move ahead as fast as we might have done in the personnel field.

At the end of the second year of the Christie Hospital NHS Trust the single most satisfying aspect of the trust's existence was the knowledge that we had given the tax payer so much better value for money for the health service resources available to us. At the same time we have delivered a better standard of service to even more patients and this was achieved by a better motivated staff and by an organisation which had a much clearer idea of its future direction. The continuing challenge is to maintain the pace of change and to support the commitment and energy which trust status has released. The wider challenge is whether a government-controlled and cash limited system can withstand the demands of provider units throughout the NHS functioning in this way.

8   Purchaser–provider relationships: current practice and future prospects

Peter Spurgeon

Introduction

There would undoubtedly be much debate as to which of the many reforms introduced into the health service over the past two to three years has had greatest impact or will ultimately prove to be of greatest significance. The delivery of services on the basis of agreed contracts, the option to acquire trust status, the purchaser/provider split in the commissioning and delivery of health care and the introduction of fund holding for general practitioners would probably all have their advocates. In practice and over time as each of the initiatives becomes established it will inevitably prove to be a combination of the interplay of the different strands.

Although the focus of this paper is on the purchaser/provider relationship it is important to consider, albeit briefly, the wider context as some of these forces may well prove instrumental in determining just how the purchaser/provider relationship operates. The overall philosophical motivation behind the reforms might be described as a desire to control total public expenditure and if possible substitute alternative forms of resourcing as a replacement of public input. Perhaps slightly more mundane might be a goal to see public resources allocated to health care spent and utilised in a more effective manner. Either way there are some fundamental and persuasive values at work here, most notably:

- *increased accountability* – at both institutional and personal levels public organisations have been made more directly accountable for how public money is used;

- *multiple providers* – slowly but steadily additional and

alternative providers have been encouraged to enter the previous monopoly of public provision;

- *differentiation of service levels* – no longer is the concept of universality of service paramount thus allowing a range of different standards and forms of service delivery to emerge;

- *consumer choice* – great emphasis has been given to the idea that the end user should exercise choice and therefore exert greater influence over the nature of the service available.

In summary these values express the concept of an internal market, incorporating the notion of a separation of the purchase of health care (eg the previous district health authorities) and the provision of health services (by the previous units, now largely trusts), the relationship between the two functions being mediated by the existence of service agreements or contracts.

Background forces

The manner in which this purchaser/provider relationship operates is the focus of this chapter. Inevitably this is itself going to be influenced by the historical pressures that have led to the establishment of this particular structure, and the perceptions of each of the participants as to what they are trying to achieve and how they might best meet their desired objectives.

Historically it is probably fair to say that the NHS has not been notably responsive to attempts to change it in the past. Many well intentioned manoeuvrings have been introduced and they have resulted in little more than a series of purely structural changes. On occasions this may have appeared to be an almost cynical resistance with staff seeming to ride out the storm of a particular initiative and then getting back to business as usual. This is of course unfair. Nonetheless the undoubted powerful resistance to change was based largely upon the fact that the professional view of the appropriateness of services remained dominant. Professional staff, especially doctors, have effectively blocked most previous reforms and have remained the determinants of which services shall be delivered and developed, and also how they will be provided. The NHS has been a provider dominated organisation. A simple, apparently superficial but relevant example would be the typically long waiting times to see a consultant for a clinic appointment. Stories of spending three to four hours or half a day are legion. Such a situation could not exist in a service industry where the customer was 'King'.

In the NHS patients and the public have found it extremely difficult to create an influential role. The apparent unresponsiveness of the service was not a conscious or antagonistic rejection but more the outcome of a set of predisposing factors. An excessive demand for an 'apparently free service' delivered by highly trained specialists with relatively limited alternative supply options combined to create a very one-sided situation. Ham (1991) says 'the setting up of the purchaser role provides a significant opportunity to exercise a counterbalancing force to this provider power'. Immediately we can see potential alarm bells within this description. The relationship is described in terms of power, counterbalancing force and thus a relationship full of conflict, domination and pre-eminence of one group over another is characterised. One view is that after the lack of success of previous initiatives then this rather explosive recipe may be what is required. Another faction sees this confrontational approach as largely rhetoric and ideology with the reality being a much more co-operative approach. To some extent these descriptions characterise the dichotomy of how the purchaser/provider relationship might operate. They, of course, encompass perceptions and prejudices about what has happened in the past and what now needs to be done to bring about reform. But this historical perspective does not exist in isolation. It needs to be linked to current requirements of the two functions of purchaser and provider.

Rather simplistically the purchaser function may be described as being required to

• assess the health needs of the populations served;

• appraise the options available for the delivery of these services;

• place contacts with selected providers and monitor the subsequent delivery of these services.

As Charny (1991) writes 'the purchaser should be the advocate of the resident population in terms of ensuring that care is effective, efficient, relevant and of a high standard. It is the purchaser, not the provider, which defends the patients interests'. If the purchasing authority can assess patient need properly and is then prepared to use the power of the contracting process to reflect these needs then indeed it is likely to have a significant impact upon the services available from the provider. It should too, almost for the first time, have the capacity to represent the consumer in the critical decisions about the nature, pattern and balance of available health care services.

The notion of placing and withdrawing contracts is of course the weapon of the purchaser and is also the essence of the internal market implied by the reforms. Nichol (1991) describes the key features of the market orientated reforms as a) the ability of the purchaser to represent consumer choice by setting standards and targets free of the conflict of interest that existed when they were also responsible for the supply of health care; and b) the right of purchasers to place contracts as and where they feel the interests of the population will be best served. He specifically uses the phrase 'good performance is rewarded, poor performance is penalised'. Here one can see the 'market' come into focus: there will be winners and there will be losers as a consequence of the operation of market forces.

Much attention has been focused upon the purchasing of health care as it is a new function and its aims, patterns of working are still evolving. For the provider community the changes are still considerable, perhaps greater in the long run, but they appear less dramatic initially. The providers, whether existing directly managed units or increasingly NHS trusts, are still concerned with the delivery of health care as they were before the separation of purchaser and provider. By and large they still receive the same type of patients, offer the same type of service and employ the same staff. Thus there is the illusion of less dramatic change.

However, all these services are now part of a contractual system involving potentially a range of possible purchasers. The priorities for a provider within the market structure outlined above must be a) to secure sufficient contracts – whether DHA purchaser or GP fundholders, to cover their costs and b) to manage their workload to ensure that they meet contract targets, neither under or over-achieving on the specified activity levels. Although simply stated these two objectives imply major changes for provider units. Firstly their whole financial viability is based upon being able to gain enough work. As competition and rationalisation of services proceeds so this single goal of survival becomes a major challenge. The second objective necessitates a number of internal managerial changes so that activities for each contract can be accurately monitored. Obviously information systems to enable this to be achieved become a priority. But there is a more persuasive cultural challenge, and opportunity, involving various strands such as bringing professional staff into the management process, examining the necessary balance of staff to provide services, potentially negotiating new jobs and salary structures outside existing national arrangements and developing competitive strategies incorporating price and quality criteria to ensure their own particular services are seen as appropriate and purchasable by their potential customers.

There are then formidable agenda on each side of the purchaser/ provider relationship. As each group learns more about their own role so they will increasingly seek to operate the relationship to achieve their objectives. It is still early days to provide prescriptive guidelines as to how purchasers and providers should interact. Nonetheless both groups are active now and thereby some models are evolving, although they are models largely driven from a practical, necessity base. A number of issues are emerging too as the market-place develops and these are likely to impact upon the nature of future relationships between purchasers and providers. We will now examine a number of these factors.

Practices

Despite the public advocacy of a clear separation in purchaser/ provider relationships, as part of the internal market development, there have been two major factors detracting from increased clarity in these new structures.

Initially there was considerable ambiguity between districts (purchasers) and units (providers) as to just how they should operate the separation. During the first couple of years of the reforms the number of trusts was relatively small and so the majority of providers were directly managed units, meaning that although they were solely concerned with providing health care via contracts received from purchasers they were still ultimately responsible to their own district healthy authority. Indeed unit general managers in directly managed units had a direct line management relationship to the district general manager with the latter also being responsible to the regional health authority for the performance (especially financial performance) of the units in his/her district. Thus those placing contracts were also responsible for the people delivering on those contracts. It is hard to see how a purchaser in these circumstances would act in such a way as to jeopardise his/her own units viably even if the interests of the population generally might have been served.

It became apparent that the whole model of the reform was in fact predicated on the establishment of NHS trusts at the provider level. In the interim a number of DHAs (purchasers) evolved different positions on the dimension of degree of separation. The more extreme views were expressed as purchasers largely disowning the units, encouraging them to manage their own affairs and to proceed towards trust status as soon as possible. This 'hands-off' approach was true to the spirit of purchaser/provider separation but was in danger of engendering a disturbing sense of ambivalence in the purchaser chief executive who remained accountable for unit performance. At the other extreme there were those who continued much as before with the district managing the unit and working together to define contracts and services.

The contracts placed between purchaser and provider tended to reflect the philosophical stance taken in that some contracts emphasised the split by identifying elements like penalty clauses or referring to 'soliciting alternative providers'. Indeed some authorities set explicit targets for themselves to identify alternative supplies and thereby started to create the competitive environment. Other contracts were written in a more co-operative spirit and largely built around what the provider unit was capable of delivering. This ambiguity in the purchaser/provider relationship is gradually disappearing as more units acquire trust status and also as purchaser authorities merge thus removing some of the old parochial loyalties.

The second 'slow down' factor reflected the Government's own nervousness about the impact of the internal market. Concern to achieve a 'smooth take-off' has produced legislation and edicts to retard the action of potential market forces. Ham (1992) has suggested that progress on the principal competitive elements underpinning the market has been slow. He argues that purchasers have been pre-occupied with developing managerial arrangements for the purchasing process and with establishing their new relationship with provider units and GPs in their area. Also purchasing chief executives have been anxious about their own position as mergers proceed. Finally, contracts during the initial phase of contracting have largely been block contracts and on central advice based upon historical patterns of service. The consequence has pretty much been steady state containing hardly any radical departures from traditional service patterns.

Markets, structure and power

The two factors described in the previous section have tended to slow down the evolution of the purchaser/provider relationship. However, as the reforms have developed generally a number of issues have emerged concerning the nature of the market, the power balance between purchasers and providers and specific aspects of how purchasing is developing.

For some, market forces are the process by which resources are allocated. However, this is a rather extreme view of the process of competition. It is perhaps only in conditions of virtually perfect competition that the market will be efficient in an allocative sense. With regard to health care as a good there are some important discrepancies in its characteristics as far as the theory of competition is concerned. Perhaps the most notable is the concept of information asymmetry (Arrow 1963) where the doctor (supplier) and patient (customer) are markedly different in their capacities to determine the effectiveness of any proposed provision. A high degree of competition would normally see a similarly high level of transactions, with some degree of trial and error within the purchaser behaviour. This is manifestly not the case with health care.

Debate about the internal market, especially of those opposed to the concept, has tended to focus rather unfairly on a more extreme highly competitive version of a market. The implications of a more constrained market are rather less controversial. As von Otter (1991) suggests the competitive influence in health care provision is aimed at securing:

• greater internal efficiency of provider organisations;

- greater responsiveness of service provision to patients' preferences;

- increased managerial effectiveness.

Thus we see how the purchaser operating within a market could have a significant impact upon the operations of the unit in terms of its efficiency and upon the managerial culture existing within the unit.

A further example of how the advance of purchasing will impact upon providers may be seen in the process by which purchasers attempt to assess health needs. There are of course problems here in the definition of need but accepting this, it is of course a main focus for the public health director involving the use of epidemiological data. One component of this will have major impact upon the nature of services delivered by provider units. The health service has largely grown via a sort of incremental pressure, expanding services by a small percentage each year. This has meant that it has tended to gauge progress by the level of inputs. The future for purchasing lies in moving away from this approach to one of assessing health outcomes as a result of the health care it purchases. Through this process the purchasing authority will be making better informed judgements about its priorities, assess whether it is improving the health status of the population or not and then consider whether a particular service should be retained, modified or abandoned. Here of course is the obvious interaction with the provider for it is here that service patterns may be changed significantly, perhaps prompting major re-structuring within the provider unit.

There are of course a number of very dynamic power relationships at play as this process unfolds. It has been stated earlier that the NHS has been a provider dominated organisation and that the reforms, in part, are about redefining aspects such as patient choice and influence. This will be operationalised in the market-place by the allocation, or not, of contracts. How viable is this concept in health care? In London and some other large cities there may well be over provision of hospital beds, especially as new technology changes the pattern of in-patient care. There may well be arguments for rationalisation or even closure. However, in more rural settings or in the average district with a single district hospital the option of withdrawing a contract still seems a long way off. Are there alternative providers within a reasonable distance? Will patients travel to this location? – early evidence suggests they are very reluctant. If contracts for a particular service are withdrawn what will be the repercussions for the viability of the local hospital or unit. Can community care at a local level be properly co-ordinated with contracts placed in a range of secondary care locations?

Many of the opportunities of purchasing are based upon the assumption that the purchaser represents the consumer and that the purchaser has a choice as to where to place contracts. The second element is varyingly true in different locations. In reality the provider retains considerable power in determining what can be delivered and at what cost or quality. There is no point in the purchaser specifying contract conditions that cannot be met or in damaging the main provider if alternative sources present access problems and are unpopular with consumers. Therefore despite the opportunities for change the constraints are such that this will in fact be quite gradual with purchaser and provider agreeing to move to different standards or different patterns of service. Only in certain circumstances will market forces be able to operate directly on provider units.

If purchasers were able to place and withdraw contracts how would providers respond? Clearly one of the new skills for provider organisations is that of competitive marketing and responding to the needs or wishes of their customers. It may be that one response is greater specialisation. It is a natural product of the market-place that providers identify a need, match it with a particular strength and through specialisation become the best provider of the service. More specialist hospitals may therefore be part of the future. Evidence from the USA suggests that outcomes from specialist units are better for patients. However, at the same time intense competition has led to over resourcing and waste through hospitals having to acquire technology to present a high profile image. This issue may lead providers to an alternative and rather different looking response, that of merging. Again as market forces squeeze resources a natural private sector reaction is for providers to merge to provide greater strength and security. Within health care it is likely that this response will also occur perhaps allowing one of the merged units to operate as a specialist unit and thus play to its strengths.

One of the arenas that is emerging as an important feature of purchaser/provider relationship is that involving GPs and GP fundholders as a third point of a triangular relationship. Undoubtedly GPs have emerged as a major factor in whether contracts are placed with a provider or not (Appleby et al, 1991). This recognition is creating a different relationship between GPs and hospital consultants with the latter beginning to recognise their dependence upon the goodwill of GPs to recommend patients rather than the previous situation where patients seemed almost to be accepted onto a consultant's list as a favour. The pivotal position of GPs in the referral process has meant that there is a need for greater contact, collaboration and discussion as to the nature of services that should be available. Some purchaser/provider structures have resulted in GPs and consultants agreeing a set of treatment protocols such that the GP can decide to treat the patient directly rather than opt for the referral. Thus GP and consultant through their dialogue are beginning to reshape the nature of the service patients receive. There is a clear parallel here to the nature of the discussions purchasers and providers in general need to have as they agree to move to new delivery patterns.

However, this pressure is not always comfortable and can result in some difficult ethical dilemmas for the provider organisations in particular. Purchaser DHAs have been required to meet certain waiting list targets and there is evidence that the number of long-wait patients has been reduced. However, it is also apparent that the movement forward of the long-wait patients may have happened at the expense of other patients who although waiting for a shorter period may be more severe cases. Doctors in provider units have therefore felt that clinical priorities have been distorted thus introducing some conflict and tension into the goals of the purchaser and provider. The former responding to a national pressure to reduce lists and the provider responding to the need to fulfil contracts. The position is likely to exacerbate as GP fundholding expands for it is clear that they will as a group control a significant sum of money. As the money is removed from the DHA purchaser so the provider will need to respond to the GP fundholder demands. This raises the prospect (already a reality for some organisations) that GP fundholders because they have the resources may be able to a) secure a faster access to service for their patients than other GPs and that b) in doing so they may again promote the interest of less urgent cases to the detriment of the more severe who cannot be treated as the DHA has no further funds to pay for them. If this fundamental principle of the NHS is not to be infringed there will need to be either very close dialogue between DHA purchasers, GP fundholders and providers or some form of appropriate legislation.

Future prospects

It is likely that the competitive element of the internal market will increase over time. However, there do seem to be some logical implications of this process which may or may not reflect the goals of the reforms. For example even in a trust based provider sector there are a number of important constraints upon market forces in health care (Spurgeon, 1993). These critical factors are:

- inter-dependence of clinical specialities;
- viability of a hospital unit;
- geographical considerations and
- political acceptability.

An aggressive, 'shop-around' purchaser is unlikely to find that all the services in hospital A are consistently better than those in hospital B. More realistically, whether the criteria used is price, quality, access or whatever, it is probable that there will be an uneven picture with some specialties better than others. The competitive model would favour the dispersal of contracts to maximise the purchasers' advantage. However, a hospital unable to maintain its range of services may not be viable financially or medically (in terms of training provision for junior doctors or links between specialties). The logic of this purchaser dominated market is that the non-viable hospital either specialises or closes. How will this fit with the total pattern of provision within a region? What sense is there in closing a hospital serving a large rural area and what might be the reaction of local politicians to the proposed closure? All these factors point to the need for a highly co-operative market structure where purchasers and providers work closely together to agree changes over time, and also work with the regional health authority to ensure that market driven movements in health provision are compatible with the overall provision within the region.

Some recent work across three regions suggests that there is a general movement towards more collaborative relationships between purchasers and providers. Ham & Spurgeon (1992) suggest that contracts are a rather clumsy tool and that the more important mechanism for improving service performance is the relationship established between purchaser and provider. This is especially so as purchasers merge and perhaps as a consequence become more remote and removed from local services. Close working relationships between large purchasers and more locally focused provider units are essential to maintain relevant service provision.

It is clear that stand-off antagonistic purchaser/provider relationships far from producing cost-effective health care can be disruptive and inefficient. There is a need for increasing maturity in the relationships so that there is co-operation between purchaser and provider to ensure effective resource usage. This is most obviously apparent when considering how provider units can progress new medical techniques or plan for longer term developments. As the current yearly contracts are formulated there is little chance that a provider unit could run the risk, or indeed carry the cost, of research and development work to pursue a new treatment technique. There must be longer term agreements encouraging entrepreneurship, efficiency and innovation. Southampton Health Commission in the Wessex Region has instituted monthly strategic exchanges with local NHS trusts and is working with the University Medical School to identify low health benefit services and potential innovations that could replace them. It is vital that this sort of innovation as well as evaluation of services is collaborative since it is largely the provider who has the medical expertise. If we are to ensure some balance in power then purchasers must join with providers in considering new techniques. One would expect to see the emergence of more longer term contracts over a number of years so that provider units can not only invest in research and development but also plan their service provision appropriately. Of course this relationship must not become cosy and complacent. A healthy tension should exist but this should not be manifested in terms of 'you will do it or else'.

The GP fundholders, as purchasers, perhaps offer the most difficulty to providers in planning for the future. As an increasingly major purchaser (especially in consortium) they have the power to destabilise a provider unit. At times this may not necessarily be intentional but simply their tendency to seek short term contracts and to respond to their own patient demands rather than assessed patient need. A major challenge to the service, and to the purchaser/provider relationship, is how to integrate GP fundholders into the notion of planned, needs based, strategic purchasing. Wessex RHA have taken a lead here by asking DHA purchasers to take on responsibility for GP fundholders in their area. The objective is that through discussion and contact DHA and GP fundholders purchasing decisions can be aligned.

Finally the need for very close purchaser/provider relationship is emphasised through problems experienced in the 1992–3 financial year with many providers having to reduce activity because they had fulfilled contracts earlier than planned. There is a need for close monitoring of activity on contracts so that income and activity can be matched. This offers purchasers the option of offering incentives for excellent performance and providers the chance to utilise their resources effectively and maximise their income. Ultimately the positive, collaborative purchaser/provider relationship advocated here is in the interests of patients and the public as change in health care is introduced more rationally and smoothly.

References

Appleby, J., Little, V., Ranade, W., Robinson, R., and Smith, P. (1991) 'Implementing the Reforms: A National Survey of District General Managers Birmingham: NAHAT.

Arrow, K. J. (1963) 'Uncertainty and the Welfare Economics of Medical Care', *American Economic Review*, **53**.

Charny, M. (1991) *A Share in Health* Bath: Ralph Allen Press Limited.

Ham, C. (1992) 'Managed Competition in the NHS: Progress and Prospects', paper presented to Manchester Statistical Society (March).

Ham, C. and Spurgeon, P. (1992) 'Effective Purchasing', HSMC Discussion Paper 28, The University of Birmingham

Ham, C. (1991) 'It isn't hurting it isn't working', *Marxism Today*, July pp14–17

Nichol, D. (1991) Opening Address in Hunter, D. J. (eds) *Paradoxes of Competition for Health Leeds: Nuffield Institute for Health Services Studies.*

Spurgeon, P. (1993, in press) 'Managing the Internal Market' chapter
in Ian Tilley (ed) *Managing the Internal Market*, Paul Chapman
Limited.

von Otter, C. (1991) 'The Application of Market Principles to Health
care' in Hunter, D. J. (ed) *Parades of Competition for Health* Leeds:
Nuffield Institute for Health Service Studies.

9 The impact of trusts in the management of the NHS

Eric Caines

Promises, promises . . .

Many were the promises, explicit and implicit, made to NHS managers at the time when health ministers and the Management Executive were selling the 'Working for Patients' (DH, 1989) reform package to a largely suspicious Service. Leaving aside the introduction of Griffiths-style management, it was the third major reorganisation of the NHS in 20 years and given the radical instincts of Kenneth Clarke it looked like being the daddy of them all. But as with any change, there were some brave souls who not only welcomed the proposed changes but were prepared to go out on a limb to turn them into reality. And it was this band of brothers and sisters who eventually put their organisations forward – often after considerable local strife and personal sacrifice – as prospective first wave trusts. They were the project managers initially, shaping the trust applications, bringing professional colleagues on board and conducting local consultations on the applications. Their profile was high and they came together at regular intervals, under the aegis of the Headquarters Trust Unit, for guidance and more particularly, for mutual support. Most of them, but not all, subsequently became the chief executives of the trusts they had nursed into life.

What was it that excited and stimulated this group to such a marked degree? What was it that led them to be prepared to put their organisations into the firing line, with all the turmoil and upheaval which that would bring, and their own futures at risk, when the rest of the Service was deciding that it was safer to sit on the sidelines and await the outcome of the impending General Election when the overall initiative might be entirely lost? Some of the reasons were apparent at the time, others have become clearer with the passage of time.

Getting 'out from under' regions

One major factor, which provides some sort of insight into the way the Service had been managed previously, was a very strongly felt need on the part of many at the sharp end – the future providers – to escape from regional control and, as they saw it, from the oppressive top-down management practised in what many regarded as the biggest bureaucracy in Europe. The pre-reform NHS was a command and control organisation driven from the top with, as it must have seemed from the bottom, endless levels of management all drawing authority from the point at which services were delivered. This amazingly strong compulsion to 'get out from under' regions, as it was frequently put, was evidence, if evidence were needed, of the frustration felt by many general managers at unit level at the hedging around of their personal responsibility for delivering services to patients with a web of bureaucratic controls, the rationale for many of which was difficult to identify.

Naturally, this was not a view which Regions shared, and they will now doubtlessly regard themselves as having delivered up to Ministers at the time a viable First Wave. Nevertheless, the resentment they felt at having, in many cases, key units seeking to fly the coop was often palpable. But the Secretary of State kept on repeating that, henceforward, Trusts would be accountable directly to the centre, which position was re-asserted uncompromisingly at the time when, as the Second Wave came along, it was being suggested that the growth in the number of Trusts would render the central role untenable and necessitate the re-imposition of some form of Regional control. The strength of this restatement of the position on accountability was what led to the acrimony between the Secretary of State and the Trust Federation when the further increase in Trust numbers occasioned by the emergence of the Third Wave again caused the question of whether the centre would not need their monitoring function to be delegated to an 'intermediate tier' to be reopened. This new nomenclature was seen by most trusts as a simple euphemism, it being widely believed that trusts were to be 'handed back' to regions. Whether this will happen has not yet been finally resolved but trust chief executives are fearful that it is part of a hidden agenda.

'Money follows patients'

What came to be regarded by some as a broken promise, but was never more in fact than a misunderstanding of how the Health Service was, and was going to continue, to be funded – or perhaps it was wishful thinking that things might be different in future – was the principle which lay at the heart of the reforms that money would follow patients. Somewhat surprisingly, this was taken by many, including many doctors, to mean that however many patients were treated money would be available to support the workload. This could never have been true, of course, other than in the sense that what some might gain through increased throughput (which was not necessarily the same thing as increased efficiency) others would lose.

It is strange, as one looks back, to believe that anyone could have thought, in effect, that the reforms meant that there would be no future overall limit on NHS resources. Well into the first wave, however, managers and doctors could be heard complaining that they were treating and could continue to treat increasing numbers of patients – anyone who turned up in fact – but that unless they were given more money than was included in their contracts they would have to put the brakes on. As events turned out, this is what they have had to do in each of the first two years of the reforms. The 'last-quarter crisis' has become a familiar feature of the NHS and it is still seen by many not as a commentary on the level of overall funding, or their ability to manage work across the year, or as an expression of the mismatch between workloads and staffing levels, but as a real disincentive, preventing them from doing as much as they could, while waiting lists lengthen.

End of the famine?

A separate strand of the generalised expectations surrounding resourcing related to the future provision of capital. The logic which developed in many minds was that the upgrading of physical facilities or even the building of new hospitals, through external funding, would give trusts an edge in the market and would allow them to attract more patients and hence generate more income. Indeed, some managers saw the reforms as providing them with the response to the substantial bids they had been submitting – and had been having rejected – for additional capital over very long periods. Some even tried to make the submission of their trust applications conditional upon understandings being given that the capital they had been seeking would be made available on their becoming trusts. Again, this was never going to be the case. Given the continuing future limitations on revenue, ministers were not going to allow locally generated capital developments which could not be supported by revenue income streams.

As things have developed, it now appears to many that the position in relation to the allocation of capital is essentially no different from what it has always been. Providers have to convince purchasers that they should be prepared to support new capital developments with future contract income which, in effect, leaves it to the purchaser to decide the directions in which capital should flow. And when an agreed large scale development takes most of the available capital in a region, the capital funds famine which then follows is as bad for most providers as it ever was.

These misreadings about future resourcing apart, the main thrust of the reforms, with the emphasis which they placed on the achievement of improved performance within a freer management regime, was well understood by those who relished the prospect of greater personal responsibility and the opportunity to embrace a true leadership role rather than a narrowly defined management role.

New tensions and new freedoms

Through the medium of the internal market – which separated purchasing and providing – the reforms introduced the idea of survival through performance. Hospitals which provided an effective service, defined in terms of volume, cost and quality would thrive and would attract more business; those which performed less well in those terms would be at risk and might not survive in the longer term. This at least was the theory and, at the time, most managers did not question the possibility that if they did not perform to acceptable standards, their units might actually go out of business in the longer term. Whilst it was always doubtful whether ministers would find it acceptable to see a hospital go to the wall as a direct result of market pressures, most managers saw it as one of the natural consequences of the reforms.

There was to be nowhere for the poor performers to hide. The only source of income would be direct either from district purchasers or from GP fundholders. Purchasers would be expected to try to get the best value for money on behalf of patients, exerting pressure over providers as the means of doing so. Purchasing power was to be the order of the day and whilst some providers felt threatened the first wave chief executives, almost to a man and woman, felt stimulated by the opportunity to operate in a more bracing environment, particularly since the other major component of the reforms was the provision of wide-ranging and statutorily underpinned freedoms from central control which left their survival in the new market to be determined by their own efforts. No longer were they to be trapped in a cats cradle of central rules and regulations. In future they would be able to take for themselves decisions, principally in relation to the use of human and financial resources, which had previously been reserved to one or other of the higher tiers of NHS management.

Steady state

The first cloud on the horizon appeared in the form of the declaration of a 'steady state' for the first year's operation of the reformed Service. No risks were to be taken either with the operation of the market or the exercise of the new freedoms and flexibilities. An election was in the offing; political risks were to be avoided and since, in the NHS, management risk invariably equals political risk, management risks were also therefore to be eschewed. But since the loss of the election would probably have meant the abandonment of many of the key aspects of the reforms, the Service went along with 'steady state' and despite being used shamefully as a political football, avoided major disasters, in which respect the availability of significant amounts of additional money was of material assistance.

Full steam ahead?

But the election having been won and the future of the reforms and of Trusts safeguarded, the expectations were that it would be full steam ahead and that the enterprise which had had to be restrained could now be released. But politics took a hand again and with the new Government under siege on the Maastricht Treaty and their handling of their pit closure programme, and with the economy worsening day by day resulting in a forced exit from the ERM, it was imperative that new controversy about the NHS should not be allowed to arise. Risk avoidance, therefore, again became the order of the day. It seemed to many that the marching orders which the new Secretary of State must have been given on assuming office could only have been to 'keep the lid on the NHS'. At least it was difficult to judge her actions in any other way.

What sort of market?

To take the internal market first: from day one, there have been and continue to be deep divisions at political and senior management levels about how the market should be allowed to develop. One school of thought believes that it should be encouraged to develop as a free market and that it should only be regulated when it seems that the provision of core services to particular communities might be squeezed out by competitive pressures. Such an approach, it is argued, would stimulate efficiency through competition and would lead purchasers, in areas where there is no competition at present, to seek to introduce it through such means as increased purchasing from the private sector. Essentially this approach looks only to regulate when regulation is absolutely necessary. It recognises that there may be circumstances in which, to put it at its most extreme, it may not be possible to let a hospital go out of business; it also recognises, however, that where services can be provided otherwise, a hospital should not be kept in business if it proves inefficient.

The other approach, whilst retaining the formal purchaser/ provider split, essentially removes much of the competitive element from the internal market by using purchasing money to ensure that the worst consequences of market pressures are avoided. This is managing the market in its true sense. This approach which approximates very closely the pre-reform top-down planning approach, looks to take the edge off the sharp consequences of competition by, for example, keeping contingency funds at both district and regional levels for use where providers run into difficulties through poor management, under-performance or lack of control. Such an approach, which is the one broadly being followed at present, undermines the belief that providers in the new NHS have to stand on their own feet and live entirely within their contract income. It gets somewhere near the old 'back pocket' approach.

The difference between the two approaches is like driving a car downhill with the brakes on and only letting them off when it feels safe to do so (the planning approach), or letting it freewheel and applying the brakes only when it looks as if it might run out of control (the market approach). The essential difference, in relation to effecting the steep change in performance which the reforms must surely have been intended to bring about, is that under the market approach the car travels much further much more quickly and has a chance of reaching its destination (wherever that might be). Under the planning approach progress is limited, much less is achieved and the purposes of change are obscured.

In its pre-reform shape, the Service essentially ran on a system of perverse incentives. The good performers would generally have to make do with less – they did not need it; the poor performers, whilst incurring some higher-level odium, would generally be helped out of the district's or region's 'back pocket'. What was the point of trying to do more and better and what did it matter to not do very well at all? The reforms were intended to turn this situation around and enable the Service to run on real incentives.

The expectation had been that there would have been an early shift in purchasing patterns as the better performers started to increase their market share. But there are few signs so far of movement in the overall shape of the market; there is little overt comparative information which allows purchasers to make informed choices and, worst of all, from the providers point of view, contracting is still based by and large on block contracting which leaves them feeling exploited and still living in the old world.

Managing through contracts

A tendency which many providers regard as an insidious attempt to widen the purchaser role to an unacceptable degree has been the increasing practice of inserting in contracts, terms designed to compel providers to fulfil their contractual commitments in a particular manner. Most providers believe that purchasers should be concerned with the 'what' and not the 'how' and that attempts to define the means whereby contractual bottom lines should be achieved is an unwarranted intervention in provider management prerogatives. The creative tension which the purchaser/provider split was intended to generate has to be based, it is argued, on an understanding of the respective roles of the two parties to the relationship. All that can be said at present, reinforced by a number of recent studies, is that in many cases something akin to an uneasy truce exists. Some hope that central guidance will inject a new and purposful sense of direction. All the indications are, however, that a similar degree of confusion about what contracting really means exists at the centre as can be identified elsewhere.

A glimmer of a real market?

Providers are, however, taking the bull by the horns in relation to marketing their services to an increasing number of GP fundholders from whom many trusts now derive a significant proportion of their income. For their part, fundholders are also beginning to drive hard bargains in the search for better services for their patients. This growing awareness on the part of trusts of the key role of fundholders and their rapidly growing expertise in relation to exploiting their new strengths provided the best example which can be found at present of the emergence of a real health market.

Who wants to be a purchaser?

In broad terms, district purchasers are still regarded as being the poor relations of trusts with regard to the availability of skills and an understanding of what they are supposed to be doing, which is not surprising given that many senior purchasers feel that they were simply 'washed up' on the purchasing shore as the more dynamic of their colleagues scrambled after and into chief executive posts in trusts in the early days of the reforms. Two years on, however, the challenges inherent in purchasing are now beginning to be appreciated and the hope must be that as the size of the challenge becomes ever more apparent, more and more people will want to take it up.

By extension, it needs to be decided at some point in the relatively near future what new career patterns senior NHS managers ought to be required to follow. With the flattening of the structures which the introduction of purchasing and providing has brought about, a trust chief executive has essentially nowhere else to go in the Service, other than to another trust, if he wishes to remain in providing. A district purchasing chief executive might still aspire, as he probably did in the past, to become a regional general manager though even this avenue of promotion may be cut off if regions disappear as a result of district mergers and amalgamations with FHSAs which gives districts the capacity to handle strategic purchasing planning for themselves. What seems unavoidable is that a career path embracing stints of work in both purchasing and providing organisations will become the preferred and acceptable route to the top, but the implications of this in relation to the maintenance of purchaser/provider tension should not be under-estimated.

If the health market is adrift in the sense that it is not clear to either purchasers or providers in which direction it is intended that it should be developed the approach to making the best use of staff is in total disarray.

But what about the staff?

The staff of the NHS have never been effectively managed, principally because managers have never had the authority to manage them. In relation to the handling of staff, the NHS has been a vast, centralised bureaucracy. Personnel policies and pay levels have all been decided through a variety of central mechanisms and adherence to them has been strictly policed from the centre. As a result of this oppressive top-down approach, there has grown up in the NHS a total dependency culture in relation to anything to do with staff. It is this, more than any other reason, which has prevented NHS trusts taking advantage of the freedoms and flexibilities which were given to them as part of the reform package. This was a once-in-a-lifetime opportunity. For the first time in more than 40 years, the prospect of escaping from the review body and/or Whitley systems on pay and from central policy dictates on how to treat staff was a real possibility. The opportunity could simply have been taken or trusts could have been made to take it. There could either have been wholesale locally agreed moves away from centrally imposed terms and conditions, which would have fatally undermined the national pay bodies and the role of the department of health personnel divisions or, after a period of notice, the pay bodies could have been disbanded. This would have forced trusts to set their own pay and personnel policies.

Neither of these has happened. Trusts have moved extremely tentatively towards the creation of new employment packages for their staffs and ministers have not been prepared to withstand the fuss which the unions and staff associations would undoubtedly have made if the pay bodies had been disbanded by central diktat.

Lost opportunities

The pity is that the expectation that this would happen, certainly so far as the Whitley Councils were concerned, was extremely high about a year ago. Indeed, it had almost become the accepted wisdom and the unions were gearing themselves up seriously to handle the push towards the local negotiation of terms and conditions. Little has happened, however, and they must be very puzzled about why it has not.

The best opportunity of all to shift the emphasis from the centre to the field in these areas arose when the Government imposed its pay policy in the autumn of 1992, at which time it was open to Health Ministers to say to the NHS that there was to be little or minimal growth in the total pay bill over the coming year and that pay increases could only be awarded to staff if measurable productivity increases could be achieved and demonstrated. These would not have been the spurious productivity deals of the past, which usually resulted in additional pay increases being simply given away to staff, but deals based essentially on getting more work done with fewer staff. But instead of telling the NHS that, in the strained economic circumstances which prevailed, it had to learn to stand on its own feet and earn through its own efforts whatever pay increases it wanted to award, ministers chose to fall back on the awful principle of evenhandedness, which cripples the Service in relation to the promotion of excellence.

The reality now has to be faced, that the opportunity to get rid of the Whitley Councils and review bodies has probably gone for at least the next five years. The present pay policy has a year to run and may or may not be extended for another year. But even if it is not extended, the scrapping of the review bodies and Whitley Councils would fail to be effected in the run-up to the next election, given that a lengthy period of notice would have to be given to enable the field to gear itself up to take over the existing central functions. This will not be a risk which ministers will be prepared to take, which means, in effect, that this particular boat has been well and truly missed. The NHS should not now complain if it finds its freedom of maneouvre over pay and personnel policies to be increasingly hedged around over the next few years. The Service has not had the guts nor the skills to take what was on offer and it should not now cry over spilt milk.

But there is some good news . . .

In one area, however, great gains have been made. In relation to the way staff are used unstoppable forces have been released. What staff do and how they do it in the NHS has, in effect, been govered by the representative staff bodies in that the way work has been packaged into specific jobs has been determined over the years by a process of negotiation between these bodies and management. The boundaries of jobs have become rigidly set and seen as something to defend by the staff interests. Any movement has only been possible if accompanied by an additional payment or a new allowance. Against the interests of NHS managers who, to meet an ever-changing situation on a daily basis, need as much flexibility as possible in the way they use their staffs, the agreements on pay and grading have been policed and enforced by the Department of Health. Only since the introduction of the reforms, has this rigid position begun to be challenged, in the teeth of fierce opposition from the staff interests, particularly the Royal College of Nursing – not surprisingly, since nurses make up half of the total NHS workforce, and are being most affected by these changes.

In simple terms, what is happening is that managers are beginning to insist that staff concentrate on what they are trained to do. Thus, nurses, who are now being trained almost to degree standard, are being required, in many places, to spend more of their time on clinical practice and less on general ward duties which, in the past, have wastefully accounted for almost two thirds of the total nursing effort. Managers increasingly want value for money from their trained workforce and are not prepared to pay staff to do work which others could do at less cost and, it has to be said, in most cases just as effectively. Indeed, the reduction in the number of support workers on wards benefits everybody. Patients get improved clinical attention from nurses who spend more time using their professional skills and feel better looked after in simple care terms by support workers who are generally there when needed.

As one door shuts . . .

It would be comforting to be able to think that as some doors close, new doors are opening in terms of the availability of opportunities to carry the reforms forward, not so much to any precise letter but in keeping with the original spirit. Such comfort is difficult to find, however, and trust chief executives and others, who nailed their colours to the reform mast, must now be wondering what has really changed. The organisational topography has changed but the better life in the new world is not evident. They are having in fact to live with a paradox. Resources are scarce and due to become more so. The reforms were designed to enable such a situation to be more effectively coped with.

Most people enjoy challenges and the first band of trust chief executives had that degree of boldness which ought to have left them well able to handle whatever difficulties might arise. But they needed to be left free to use their skills, experience, ingenuity and flair and the fact is that their freedoms are being more and more constrained by the centre with every day that passes. The world they inhabit is not the world they imagined it would be. It is difficult to see how the expectations they had can be revived. Indeed, as one of them observed recently, it seems that 'as one door shuts, another door closes'.

10 Trusts: the reasons to be cautious

Andrew Wall

By April 1994 the implementation of the purchaser/provider split will be all but complete. Trusts will be responsible for the management of NHS facilities across the country. Any sceptism as to the appropriateness of the new system may therefore appear to be redundant. But, as governments have sometimes learned to their cost, the NHS is never far from the public consciousness or the political arena. The media are unlikely to lose their almost obsessive interest in health care, its successes and – more copy worthy – its failures. How will trusts survive this continual exposure? Will they prove to be as successful as their advocates are claiming or are there already indications that, after all, these changes were likely to cause more problems than they solved.

Certainly the separation of providers from purchasers is by no means unusual in today's health systems worldwide. But that does not automatically validate that separation; it may be no more than fashion given the propensity of western developed countries to copy each other's political ideas. Learning from each other may seem sensible but only if what is learnt is also sensible. In the case of trusts – the exemplification of the new style health service – there are still residual doubts about the concept. But experience of the new arrangements is also adding new doubts about the capability of managers and clinicians to make the system work effectively. What would be the consequences of failure? These issues need addressing if only to endeavour to avoid the pitfalls.

Re-examining the concepts

The purchaser/provider split

Most people have accepted as a given the view expressed in 'Working for Patients' (DH, 1989), that the organisation of health will be enhanced by creating:

'an organisation in which those who are actually providing the services are also responsible for day-to-day decisions about operational matters. . . . DHAs can then concentrate on ensuring that the health needs of the population for which they are responsible are met . . .'

The assumptions behind this statement need re-examination as they are by no means self-evidently true. To begin with the division of work is simplistic. Ironically it was tried in the 1974 reorganisation when Area Health Authorities were meant to concern themselves with planning health care leaving the District Management Teams (DMT's) to get on with the business of running the service. The result was a failure and in eight short years the system was unscrambled to allow the post 1982 DHAs to be responsible for both planning and operational management. This integration of today's task with tomorrows's was further enhanced by the Griffiths general management reforms of 1984 onwards. But why did the 1974 system prove so unacceptable? The fallacy is that such separation of functions is unnatural. Simply stated, anyone at work has ideas about how their job might be improved; in other words they consider changes at the very same time that they undertake their tasks. Not everyone in an organisation will have the necessary authority to change matters but there is a natural desire to do so. Furthermore this possibility of change acts in itself as an incentive. Work is an iterative process where today's experience informs tomorrow's plans and tomorrow's plans become in their turn today's experience. There is something intrinsically unnatural therefore in separating today from tomorrow. Indeed it does not happen in practice as AHAs in the 1970s found to their cost. DMTs had very certain ideas about what they wanted to do and tended to disregard AHA plans to the extent of rubbishing them on the basis that planners divorced from the operation of the service could not possibly know what was really needed. In any case, we learn from our own experience, not other people's.

Learning is further conditioned by the success or failure of our plans. Under the new system actions and their consequences are divorced. Trusts maintain that it is not their fault that operations have had to be cancelled at the end of the year because the money has run out. On the contrary, DHAs are universally blamed for their failure to provide 'enough money'. In an effort to recover their reputation, DHAs in turn blame trusts for their inability to pace their expenditure. This mutual recrimination does little for the image of the NHS already under continual pressure from a press avid for public sector shortcomings. The public, generally, are unlikely to be in the position of judging who is in the right and who in the wrong; they can be excused for finding such public displays of disunity depressing and disturbing.

Competition

One of the justifications for the split between purchasers and providers was the belief that it facilitated healthy competition between providers as the new purchasing organisations chose between trusts and their wares. This belief, fundamental to the Conservative Party's policies over the last decade, is contestable. This is not the place to debate market principles except to question whether in the context of health care competition between providers always brings down prices and pushes up standards. The spirit of free enterprise does not lead inevitably to lower prices or better services. Indeed experience is already showing that the services bought by enterprising purchasers in the market place do not necessarily lead to improvement in care. For example, considerable anxiety has been expressed by orthopaedic surgeons that patients having hip replacements away from their home district are showing a higher complication rate. Of course, this could be an attempt to interfere in the workings of the market; a sort of restrictive practice to ensure that patients are only dealt with locally. But either way the market is found wanting: it cannot assure standards and it cannot control restrictive practices.

It has often been pointed out that market conditions do not prevail for a great number of patients; there are just not the alternatives to provision for many accident and emergency patients, for the elderly or for people with mental illness. In such cases the trusts may well have the purchaser at their mercy. Already the private sector has demonstrated how when DHAs are under pressure, providers can ask the earth. The cost of providing care for those patients with challenging behaviour has rocketed to near £100,000 per patient per year. One market lesson is that a customer under stress is likely to pay anything. A stranded motorist does not quibble about the cost of the pick up in the middle of the night in an isolated place.

But to be fair to providers, they are bound to have a business strategy which avoids financial risk as far as possible. Gone is the safety net of the District Finance Officer's ability to transfer money from one budget centre to another, gone also is the flexibility of a large budget where virement could rescue those in temporary difficulty. No wonder therefore that trusts endeavour to secure themselves against risk by incorporating a financial cushion into their negotiated prices. Simply the money is unlikely to go as far in such a regime.

Some would argue that health is not a commodity and that the there is a fundamental fallacy in endeavouring to trade as though it were. Trading concentrates on those aspects of health which are susceptible to detailed pricing – an operation, a fixed term in a hospital bed – and not on those aspects of health where the input is more difficult to measure or the outcome more extended over time: examples are health promotion or the care of disabled people.

Organisational mythology

Organisations are surrounded by myths. At one level this is an attempt to give meaning to what may appear shapeless and difficult to describe. Particular prone to myth is the question of size. 'Working for Patients' (DH, 1989) effortlessly fell into the 'small is beautiful' myth – in itself a great simplification of Schumacher's theories – in its intention that 'as much power and responsibility as possible will be delegated to local level' and in order 'to stimulate a better service to the patient, hospitals will be able to apply for a new self governing status as NHS Hospital Trusts'. It does not of course follow that delegation will produce automatically a better service. Organisational size is determined by purpose, resources, geography, function. Seldom do all these coincide to produce a requisite size: usually the 'best fit' principle will be used accmmodating some degree of compromise. But the popularity of the supposed benefits of smallness prevails and was exploited by 'Working for Patients'.

Similarly corporate identity has been said to be improved by smallness. This is to misread the evidence. The happy hospital is determined by a great deal more than its size. A hospital of 40 beds can be the unhappiest working environment if all the staff are at odds. For them there is no escape whereas in a larger institution reallocation of staff to reduce tension is possible. The porter has a very different view of the hospital from the chief executive. He may get his work satisfaction not from contributing to the common good but from exerting some power as a gatekeeper, providing prompt service to the ward sister he likes but witholding it from another sister he dislikes. To assume that everyone has the same conceptual allegiance to the trust as an entity is naive. For some professionals their commitment may be well be beyond the confines of the trust, to their profession and to the idea of the NHS as a whole. If therefore some staff only have loyalty to a segment of the hospital while others support a far wider ideal, corporate unity cannot be assumed. A sense of unity of purpose may also be challenged as each group severally defines its own status in the hierarchy often enhancing their own sense of identity by delineating the shortcomings of colleagues.

Given all this, the support for the beneficial effects of smaller organisations as exemplified by trusts looks little more than sentimental. Managing such organisations requires more sophistication if the staff within it are to feel purposeful and valued.

Freedom

Trust status has been seen as a bid for freedom. But such a word proves difficult to handle, first conceptually and secondly in application. In most situations freedom can only be described in terms of an individual's sense that he or she has the opportunity to act without constraints in a manner that his or her will determines.

Individually this may be difficult enough; for organisations it is largely impossible. The NHS is controlled by statute. Its practice is heavily regulated and indeed rightly so. Its resources are circumscribed. So where does freedom come from? What liberty can trusts claim when they are so constrained? In so far that they may succeed in enlarging their business they only do that at the cost of someone else. Indeed the concept of opportunity cost is very real: my freedom may be bought at your cost. At one level freedom is a value and therefore not to be treated as a commodity but in practical terms trusts are limited in what they can do and how they do it. What of course is being attacked is bureaucratic constraint where superiors in a hierarchy are seen as suppressing the desires and it is assumed, the talents, of those in the lower strata. But this also verges on the sentimental. In cannot be assumed that small organisations are more effective than large or that they can claim greater virtue in the way they operate. The freedom they desire is often only to rid themselves of the trappings of accountabilty. Such a wish is inappropriate in a public service. It could be argued that allowing trusts the freedom to 'own' their assets and to trade is little more than having their hand in the public's till. These assets do not belong to them. Ironically this reverses the 1948 situation when voluntary hospitals complained that the state had commandeered private assets.

The other aspect of the concept of freedom which has been much rehearsed by politicians and others is that the purchaser/provider split allows patients more choice, and thus gives them more freedom. Again it has to be said that one person's choice may be another's non choice. Hence the debate on the incipient two tier service brought about through fundholding. When, and if, all GPs become fundholders this choice will evaporate. In any case the contracting system, as many commentators have pointed out already, has reduced rather than enhanced patient choice. Responsible GPs may feel uneasy at referring patients outside contracts on the basis that an unpredictable number of extra contractual referrals will destabilise health authorities' finances and that can only lead to problems with future purchasing intentions.

Language

The language of the 'reforms' (in itself a challenging description of the changes) should make us pause. Given the need to communicate clearly and effectively any politician can be excused for relying heavily on rhetoric. But when the rhetorical devices are used to colonise the minds of the listener allowing no dissent, then the effect is more pernicious. 'Working for Patients' was launched with an unprecedented reliance on the skills of public relations experts. The document itself is prefaced by the then Prime Minister's words whose up-beat tone could have been use to describe almost anything. Resounding phrases encourage the reader to share in the vison:

> 'The National Health Service at its best is without equal . . . A skilled and dedicated staff have coped superbly . . . I am confident that all who work in it will grasp these opportunities to provide even better health care for the millions and millions of people who rely on the National Health Service.'

With this example in mind, trusts may be excused for following the same line in their submissions for trust status. As has been often, if somewhat sourly, observed, the printing industry has found a friend in the NHS changes. But are these snide comments fair or even important? It is surely reasonable that trusts along with others in commerce and industry, should use modern communications to their best advantage to help the general public to understand their message. To this end the language of the changes has relied heavily on analogy and metaphor. We have already seen how a conceptual world has been created by words such as 'freedom'. Interpreting these ideas has had to rely on analogies which seemed to fit. So the language of commerce has proved most useful. The 'market', 'competition', even 'efficiency' are key words in that world. Patients become 'customers'. But the use of these words also carries a potential danger. What if, as has already been discussed, the NHS is not a market, that competition is largely illusory, that by describing patients as customers is not always appropriate? What if the freedom the trusts desire is supported by the 'light touch' of the NHSME's Outposts rather than the 'heavy hand' of the regions?

Is the language appropriate or is public accountabilty being sacrificed to a play on words and their associated images? The metaphors of war and games have, as always, been much in evidence. From 'level playing fields' with the associated ideas of mutually agreed rules, scarcely adequate for the whole range of health care, to the 'battlegrounds' of contract negotiation, we see an attempt to limit our thoughts to contain the complexity of our activity. But this is only one step from a more sinister process whereby language is controlled itself. Initially the agreements between purchasers and providers were called 'service agreements' which was descriptive and reasonably free of associations. In due course 'contracting' became the word of choice until the government became alarmed at the commercial associations of the word and the implication that health care was becoming depersonalised by a bureaucratic processs. 'Service agreement' was recommended by the Department of Health in 1992 (DoH, 1992). But by now the damage had been done, 'contracting' it remains.

This section has gone back over some of the assumptions that have supported the introduction of the health service changes. The speed of implementation has been impressive given the widespread criticisms of the proposals both from within and without. This says much for the ability of the government to invite managers into the government's 'assumptive world' (this idea has been particularly developed by Ken Young in *Public Policy in Theory and Practice*) and make them feel at home there. Trusts and other parts of the NHS may feel that they are guests with power to leave at any time. Whether this is so relies on their own ablity to make the changes work effectively. This is by no means assured. The capability of health service managers is facing greater challenges than ever before.

Capability

Management is never good enough. In all organisations there is a feeling, voiced or not, that the quality of management is not sufficient for the task. In the NHS this anxiety is never far from the surface. With the introduction of general management from 1984 onwards, there were opportunities to recruit from a wider market of managers but people appointed from outside the NHS were not noticeably more successful than internal candidates. Nevertheless there are now renewed opportunities to appoint managers to trusts whose experience is outside the NHS. The basic justification for doing this is that an effective manager can be effective anywhere which is to espouse the idea that management is more about process than context. But to counter this view, some successful commercial organisations would feel that to be nurtured within the value system of a particular firm is a necessary prerequisite for successful management in that firm. But equally others would quote examples where an outsider rescued a flagging management from disaster.

Trust chairs could be forgiven for taking either view. What is less easy to believe is that because the system has changed: yesterday's ugly ducklings have become today's swans overnight. The characteristics which make a good manager are presumably present whatever the level of experience and whatever the context. So an effective unit general manager may well prove equally effective as a chief executive of a trust. But this assumption is perhaps too easily made. It is beginning to be apparent that this career jump is bigger than at first thought.

As UGM, the manager was accountable to the district general manager. This relationship was not just typified by the achievement of agreed objectives; in the better organisations, the relationship was more creative and more mutually supportive. As has often been observed delegation is not abdication, so that a UGM could demonstrate his or her authority and expertise fully without feeling circumscribed by being accountable to another. For those who felt frustrated, there was one answer: become a DGM and assume the responsibilities you feel yourself capable of. With the introduction of trusts many UGMs felt obliged to appear capable of this transition.

But the change involved is more substantial than they may have realised or been prepared for.

The demands upon the trust chief executive are considerable. First he or she has to learn how to work effectively with the chair and with the other non-executives. Secondly the chief executive has to provide vision and direction showing an ability to build relationships with a wide range of people and agencies. Managing the business efficiently determines the success or failure of the trust. To undertake these major tasks requires preparation but with the usually haphazard approach to management development in the NHS, many chief executives will not have had adequate opportunities to acquire the necessary skills. The experience of many people so far has been that the setting up of trusts has been accompanied by a degree of hype which leads to the suspicion that chief executives are only just keeping their heads above water. In order to protect the future of trusts, some of the problems attending managerial capability need looking at further.

Working well with a chair cannot be assumed to happen spontaneously. Clarification of roles needs to be agreed early on. What is the nature of leadership in an organisation which has two aspirants, the chief executive and the chair? Working as a member as well as the chief executive of a Board is a new experience. To be the supervisor of some of your Board colleagues is by no means easy when there are differences of opinion. The demands on the new chief executive are great. It is not enough to run a successful organisation; the chief executive must be seen as doing so in order to prove that the government's changes are a good thing. There is therefore a double burden, accountability to his or her own Trust Board but also allegiance to a government policy in a climate which has not been noted for its unforgiving nature.

It is not surprising therefore that some chief executives of trusts have relied on crude managerial devices to get through their work. The first has been an excessive reliance on rhetoric which, as has has been discussed already, bridges the gap between policy and reality. The management books which sell the most are those which personalise success and offer quick fixes as to how to join the club of the managerial elite. But the fact is that running a health care organisation is complex – arguably more so than the most other organisations – and the skills needed are not so easily come by.

What is difficult to understand therefore is why it has been assumed that the setting up of trusts would offer more chance for managerial successes than before. It would appear that the purpose – patient care – is largely the same, the colleagues are much the same, the internal structure not so very different and the constraints as rigorous as before. But it could also be argued that the trust's purpose is significantly different in that its main intention is to fulfil the contracts negotiated with purchasers and to do so to the agreed standard in return for cash. No longer do trusts have to worry about doing anything they are not paid to do. Although this may be technically true, it cuts little ice with the public whose comprehension of the niceties of the purchaser/provider split may be rudimentary.

Freedom to make decisions, often lauded by trust chief executives as one of the main satisfactions of their new role, should not been seen as freedom to ignore obligations whether these be to the patients or to the staff. It is notable that the freedom to introduce local pay bargaining, a significant feature of the reforms, has not been espoused by many trusts. Freedom as a concept, is more about how people feel than what they do.

Greater efficiency

In the popular consciousness, public service organisations are perceived as being inefficient. This is another aspect of the mythology referred to earlier. To be proved it would be necessary to undertake a wide ranging comparatative exercise. In any case this sort of discussion is beside the point. The public believe that the NHS is inefficient, the Conservative Government has in the past also believed so. Those anxious to defend the NHS have drawn a different conclusion much bolstered by comparisons with the USA. Some broad facts can be rehearsed such as the comparatatively low proportion of the GDP spent on health in the UK, and the relatively good results our clinical interventions manifest when compared internationally.

For managers, the underfunding debate is largely irrelevant; their task is to ensure that whatever funds are available are used efficiently to ensure an effective outcome. Do the reforms make that more likely to happen?

It is now possible to link activity with cash. This simple requisite of all commercial undertakings was largely absent from the NHS before; instead there was an understanding between managers and clinicians that work would be done within a global budget, sub divided into budget centres but not related in any detailed way to individual patients. Trusts are loath to work in that way even when uncertainties of demand such as in Accident and Emergency departments may offer no alternative. So universally there is a desire to move away from generalised block contracts to cost and volume and, where possible, cost per case. But what has this to do with the overall efficiency of the NHS? Indeed it could be said to lead to a state of affairs where less is done on the basis that trusts are likely, as previously noted, to avoid risk wherever possible. Furthermore the loss of flexibility with the subdividing of budgets has the potential for reducing volume. It may well be that this in turn forces trusts and purchasers to examine the more effective use of money and indeed much has been made of the shift to day surgery and to reduce fruitless returns to outpatients. But it has to be said that that sort of efficiency measure did not require the wholescale restructuring of the NHS particularly as the costs in terms of the new structures and the new processes are substantial.

At present trusts will be using at least three descriptions of cost: actual cost (if they can calculate it), contract price, and marginal cost. Managers' ability to manipulate the elements of costs is still rudimentary. Non executives complain that their trust executives are still tied to managing expenditure rather than income and that this leads to financial insecurity.

The parliamentary Opposition has not been slow to enquire into the costs of the reforms themselves. It is a simple act of arithmatic to add up the extra managerial costs associated with the new Trust Boards. The chair will be receiving a honorarium of around £20,000 and his or her non executive colleagues some £5,000 each per annum. Add to that the higher salaries of the executives and every trust represents a fixed managerial cost in excess of what was paid out previously and before any work has been done. The justification, and there is a lot of support for this view, is that the NHS is under managed and even with these additional costs still compares very favourably with any other large organisation public or private.

Nevertheless hidden within the system are the costs of contracting itself. Once the system is fully operational with not only the new purchasing authorities but also a large number of GP fundholders, the number of contracts which the average trust will have to negotiate is likely to be over 1,000 if we assume 20 specialities times 50 purchasers. The process time needed to draw up such contracts and then negotiate them is increasing particularly as the contracts themselves become more specific. In terms of ultimate benefit to the patient the cost/benefit ratio seems likely to become unacceptable: too much managerial time for too little improvement to patient care. There has already been a complaint that over 18,000 extra managerial and administrative staff have been recruited and even given some problems with transfer from one skill group to another which these figures may disguise, the increases are considerable. In order to counteract the political burden of this, the government have been forced to reduce the size of regions. Can managers prove themselves capable of running trusts without a heavy reliance on increasing management costs?

Finally in this review of the effect on managerial capability that the setting up of the new trusts has had, we should look at the intentions of 'Working for Patients' and subsequent government and Department of Health statements on the quality of the service.

Much has been made of the seeming inability of the NHS to remove its waiting lists. In vain it is pointed out that other countries may also have waiting lists but submerged in limited access to health care or bought off by higher expenditure. The waiting lists are seen as an indictment of a state run system and this is undoubtedly damaging to the NHS image both at home and abroad. Having said this, there is no intrinsic reason why the present intitatives could not have been accommodated in the old system. Indeed there were some examples where DHAs had bought health care from the private sector to reduce an unacceptable waiting list. The supporters of trusts would however maintain that trusts have an added incentive to bid for special monies to remove waiting lists and this also helps in their own internal battle to get greater command over their own medical staff, encouraging better discipline (if that is what it is.) among the consultant staff of a hospital. But in the better hospitals that process was already underway by the appointment of clincal directors. Chief executives of trusts have still some way to go to demonstrate that they are able to manage the work of medical colleagues to ensure uniformly high standards and good results. Some may feel wary of tackling such a powerful profession.

More widely, the introduction of quality across the whole organisation relied entirely on the vision and the leadership of the senior management team. There is no reason why the transformation of UGM to chief executive should suddenly make a difference. Assuring quality in depth and continuously in an organisation takes more than the writing of a quality plan and the appointment of one dedicated member of staff. It is a slow process of developing the overall consciousness of the institution or organisation to a quality orientated way of thinking. Evidence of compliance with this new approach (at least in the NHS) is as yet sketchy and the recurrent directives from the NHSME do little to reassure the public that improving quality has got beyond stage one. This is not surprising given the prevailing culture of the NHS where compliance with centrally determined objectives has never been more marked. For all the rhetoric associated with the setting up of trusts and their apparent freedom, the NHS is more centrally controlled than before.

Managerial capability can also be tested by the manner in which staff are treated. Here the experience seems to suggest that the new NHS has only been brought about by fairly Draconian means. The previously time honoured procedures for the recruitment of staff have been largely superceded by an ad hoc system said to be more in line with current commercial practice. At the senior level this commonly includes head hunting rather than open recruitment with the consequent risk to equal opportunities. In the appointment of managerial staff, the system of assessors once a safeguard against bias, is now largely ignored in favour of much more closed interviews. Freedom in this context therefore seems to be defined by the freedom to avoid what in the past and over a long period has been held to be good practice, and is still confirmed by human resource specialists to be so.

In summary therefore, the setting up of trusts has put additional burdens on managers which they were often unprepared for. The pressure on chief executives in particular and the potential isolation of their new role, has led, in many people's opinion to a drop in the standards which govern managerial practice. This may be due to outside and internal pressures, but the alleged freedom to act swiftly, to be flexible and responsive, should have minimised the effects.

Together with doubts about managerial standards is the considerable increase in administrative process which is a hallmark of the new arrangements. To date the process shows little evidence of passing a cost-benefit test in favour of patients. If all this is true the setting up of the new trusts could be seen at best as just one other way of running the health service – no better overall, but no worse. To test this view we have to look at the longer term consequences of these changes.

Consequences

The continuum of care

One of the prevailing problems facing any health care system is to ensure that the patient is in the right place for the right purpose. Failure to manage the patient leads not only to inappropriate care but also to a poor use of resources. Has the setting up of trusts had any effect on this? At one level it could be said that trusts have a vested interest in getting rid of patients at the earliest opportunity so that the risk of wasting resources by bed blocking is less likely now than before. But that is only the perspective of an acute trust. The mirror to that position is a community trust's experience of receiving a patient from a general hospital too soon thus increasing the load on community staff. Their incentive is, therefore, to ensure that patients are only accepted when they have recovered some degree of independence. Before the setting up of trusts this problem could be resolved by the appropriate managers, ward sister and community nurse, meeting and agreeing protocols. That is now far less likely. The contracting managers of both trusts are scarcely likely to allow conversations with such resource implications to take place unchaperoned. There may be situations where an acute trust is anxious to keep a patient rather than transfer or discharge them, for instance a 'high earner'. So a patient undergoing long term rehabilitation may be seen as an asset irrespective of his or her need to make progress into the community. Trust arrangements are therefore apt to put barriers across the continuum of care which are not in the interests of the patient. Even where good intentions prevail, they still have to be administered by specific agreement usually at a higher level of management than before.

Strategic development

On the face of it the new responsibility of purchasing authorities to plan the overall configuration of health care could be said to be an improvement on the previous arrangement. But to configure health care is not the same as configuring the distribution of health care facilities and it is here that the setting up of autonomous trusts may make it increasingly difficult to ensure that patients have reasonable access to what they need. This problem presents in a variety of ways. First there is now a lack of common interest between the purchasers and the providers. Providers are bound to be more interested in doing what they are good at, and what they can guarantee a market for, which is not at all the same thing as ensuring a reasonable range of services across the board. So for instance, a particular specialty may be seen as having little financial appeal in return for the amount of managerial time to be spent on running it. An example of such a service might be that for people with learning disabilities. A high degree of difficulty from multi-agency involvement together with an assertive pressure group often peopled by the clients' own families may make this a great deal more challenging than services for elderly people where patients and relatives may be more inclined to be grateful.

Even where purchasers are still able to ensure a comprehensive service, changes in the pattern of services may be more difficult to push forward. The closure of mental hospitals, long established as national policy, may now be slowed down as trusts respond to public opinion which recently has started to baulk at the inadequate arrangements for community care. With the recent changes in social security funding, such hospitals and those for the elderly may see a market opportunity which ensures their future rather than their demise.

The configuration of acute hospitals is not necessarily improved by trust status. Despite the then Secretary of State's strictures that trusts were not to be set up as a ploy to block hospital closure, it is no secret that hospitals which otherwise might have been at risk have seen trust status as a way of defending themselves. The smaller DGH, of which there over 30 in the country, are particularly likely to adopt this strategy. This limits scope for developing a new hospital plan similar to the 1962 document which would help regions and purchasing authorities to ensure that resources were developed according to need rather than as a result of popular demand and sentimental responses, the life-blood of the 'Save our Hospital' movement.

Accountability

That trusts should be so sensitive to local demand might imply that they were more accountable than before to their customers. This is not necessarily so. The official guidance sets few obligations only asking that one meeting a year be held in public. Most trusts seem likely to adopt this position on the grounds that most business being conducted by a Board is of a confidential nature concerned with the contracting, and that to have this undertaken in public would reduce the possibilities for commercial advantage. But if everyone did their business in public this particular reasoning would fall to the ground.

Another reason given for not having open meetings is that the decisions to be made are too difficult, for instance they may be concerned with limiting services. But the degree of difficulty is not in itself a justification for secrecy. It is true, however, that closed meetings do not put the same burdens on the Board and do protect them to some degree from lobbying. As the new non executive members are not representatives as such of their community this lack of visible accountability must be of concern in a public service. The new non executives, in the nature of things, come from a relatively narrow stratum of society. It could be argued that the obligation to be accountable rests more with the purchaser than with the provider because the provider's accountability is more through the business process by honouring the contract that has been negotiated. Providers however have displayed considerable nervousness to the purchaser in trying to assure themselves that their providers are capable of meeting the appropriate standards on the grounds that any intervention will be a covert attempt by the purchaser to manage, albeit obliquely, the provider. So monitoring standards, where it has been done at all, has been restricted to retrospective checking. But for the public to be assured that all is well it could be argued that purchasers should accredit providers *before* letting contracts not afterwards. Trusts have scarcely welcomed this approach as they see it as a restiction of their sense of freedom.

Confidence

It has already been said that the public have a poor understanding of the structure of the new health service and are thus unable to give a clear account of who is responsible for what. This is inherently dangerous in that public accountability cannot flourish where knowledge is so scanty. But if the public do not have detailed knowledge, they do have feelings. Progressively the popularity of the NHS, always high in the past, is being eroded year by year. This is based on the perception of the NHS received from the media which is largely adverse and on the experiences of individuals who, faced with the attitudes of staff under pressure, may be prepared not to blame those staff themselves, so much as their managers, largely unseen. In this they are not so wrong; it is an obligation of managers to provide good working conditions for staff and to support them when they are under pressure. But it could be that despite the apparent enthusiasm by the more senior managers of the NHS, the rank and file are not yet persuaded that the new system is better than the old.

The more politically aware may still, despite the frequent denials, believe that the setting up of trusts is the first step to privatisation. Whether this is the covert intention of the Government – and one must assume that it is not – the new arrangements make it easier to happen on the grounds that purchasers have no reason other than of an ideological nature, to differentiate between a private or a public provider. If the conditions of the contract can be satisfied and the price is right, a purchaser would be failing to get the best benefit if it ignored an eligible private provider. Trusts are barred from private sector status by the 1990 act itself although they are given freedoms similar to a private health contractor. The bogey of privatisation is unlikely to go away and as the public get less squeamish at the gradual but relentless dismantling of the post war welfare state, a new found pluralism which gives equal status to public and to private health providers may command public support. When and if that were to happen, the advantages of being a public rather than a private trust would be less easy to define. But equally as the pressure on the private sector also continues, some not-for-profit organisations might seek NHS trust status.

Managerial behaviour

Crucial to effective management is how the managers themselves behave. We have already seen how, despite exhortations from the Chief Executive of the NHSME, the Secretary of State and the Director of the Instite of Health Services Management, there has been a susceptability to behave in a manner which appears to have been learnt from fictional board room dramas rather than from the research of organisational behaviourists. The dichotomy between what people say and what they do can be explained in part by the fact that people have good intentions which under pressure they are unable to honour. Nevertheless the new organisations tend to encourage adversarial relationships. In a monolithic but centrally commanded organisation, a good manager imparts a set of shared values down through the staff so that work is done within a common culture, to agreed standards and in an accepted manner. Now that the average district is subdivided into several trusts, the opportunities for disagreement and for different styles are many.

It may only be the first stage in adjusting to the new arrangements but it is a matter of report that negotiations between purchasers and provider trusts have been acrimonious in many places. What is needed is a new paradigm based on partnership. As yet most managers feel unable to act in such a collaborative manner. For this the government and senior management throughout the NHS must take the blame. What they say and what they do has created a destructive climate which if left untended will make the new system virtually unworkable.

Conclusion

Has the setting up of trusts as the major plank in the Government's reforms made the NHS more or less manageable? The problems of increasing need and a more demanding public was always going to put pressure on management. But whether this particular solution will help depends on the quality of the original diagnosis. 'Working for Patients', it is commonly agreed, came about because Mrs Thatcher had become exasperated at the continual criticism of the government's handling of the NHS. Her review, conducted in private, was, we know, subject to its own internal pressures (Butler, 1992) and what started as an issue about funding ended as something rather different.

This chapter has argued that the diagnosis of organisational incompetence was never proved and it therefore follows that the measures aimed at correcting this difficulty were not necessarily well chosen. Where there has been inadequacy, other remedies could have worked just as well. An increasing grip on standard setting through professional audit; a more sophisticated management of budgets through resource management; the installation of new information systems and the prorgressive use of comparative data – all these were proceeding anyway. One thing is certain: the cost in time in endeavouring to make the reforms work has been colossal and the person in the street might be forgiven for asking whether this time, and money, could not have been better spent. This sceptism as to the efficacy of the changes has been echoed by the House of Common's own Health Committee when they said in their report presented in November 1992:

> The Department and the NHSME appear confident that they can both retain all the benefits of an integrated and strategically-planned service and simultaneously absorb all the benefits of delegated management, market forces and competition. This confidence is something that this Committee feels bound to examine against experience over the coming months and years

Scarcely unequivocal endorsement of the changes! But these health service reforms do no more than has been done before through legislation, notably in the changes in local government. It is assumed that changing the structures brings about benefits. All managers must be tempted to endorse that view, particularly as in the present case they stand to improve their own power base. But those with a greater sense of history and a greater zeal to improve the real quality of our society might feel that at best, structural change is an irrelevance, and at worst a positive threat to society's future well-being. In this context NHS trusts have much to prove.

References

Butler, J. (1992) *Patients, Policies and Politics,* Open University Press.

DoH Executive Letter 1992

Department of Health (1989) 'Working for Patients', Cmnd 555, London: HMSO.

Health Committee (1992) 'NHS Trusts: Interim Conclusions and Proposals for Future Inquiries', First Report, London: HMSO.

Young, K. (1979) *Public Policy in Theory and Practice* London: Hodder and Stoughton.

11 Forward from here: Future development

Edward Peck and Peter Spurgeon

It is not our intention to try and provide a neat resolution of the many and varied perspectives presented in this publication. To attempt to do so would be to under estimate both the complexity of the subject and the importance of being aware of the diversity of views.

Nonetheless, there are a number of themes which we feel warrant emphasis. First and foremost among these is the apparent shift in power in the NHS that the creation of NHS trusts seem to represent. This shift has at least two facets. The first shift relates to the distribution of power between the interest groups within the NHS. The view of a number of contributors is that the pursuance and possession of trust status has served to increase the authority and confidence of provider managers. This is perhaps echoed in the feeling that the initial workings of the 'internal market' have been largely provider led. As purchasing matures and GP fundholding grows there may be an increasing re-alignment of power.

The growing influence of managerialism in the NHS is underlined by the key criteria set out for the selection of non-executive directors of Trust Boards, that is, management skills. On this evidence the reforms contained in 'Working for Patients' (DH, 1989) seem to be achieving the change in culture that research on the implementation of the first Griffiths Report (1983) suggests that general management was unable to deliver. As Harrison et al (1992) conclude after a thorough review of the research literature on the impact of general management

> 'the Griffiths managerial package . . . has failed to manoeuvre general managers into a position of dominance over decisive functions of the health care market. 'Working for Patients' would appear to present provider managers with an opportunity to achieve that position of dominance both through the creation of explicit new levers of control and a further move towards managerial values in the overall culture of the organisation.'

In many successful trusts the gradual acceptance by doctors of a managerial responsibility as opposed to co-ordination may be further manifestation of the realism created by trust status.

Secondly, the reforms further reinforced the recognition by politicians of the central role of management in the successful operation of the NHS. Provider managers were engaged in the process of developing the proposals for NHS trusts in a fashion that was new for the NHS. In 1982, a Conservative Health Minister drew mirth and applause from the annual conference by referring to the 'administrative tail wagging the NHS dog'. By 1992, managers were seen as the main partners in achieving change. This partnership has not been achieved without a price for managers, particularly for those first wave chief executives who found themselves in the difficult position of being identified as champions of reform with which they were not themselves personally comfortable. Local managers have, therefore, been drawn further into the political domain than was ever previously the case. For instance, the announcement of a significant number of successful trusts became an annual political event as Mark and Scott (1992) note, 'events management is a process by which politicians, both nationally and locally, target an object for delivery by managers as proof that action has been taken'.

These themes register strongly when considering NHS trusts. They are currently much more muted when considering NHS purchasing organisations. With regard to the power of purchasers, the Health Committee (1992) 'interim conclusions' on trusts recorded that, 'our concern in the future will be to establish whether a robust mechanism exists for monitoring overall strategic provision given the level of autonomy inherent in trust status'. Trusts have undoubtedly got off to a flying start in their relationship with purchasers. Largely ignored by the department in the first two years of the reforms and victims of a haemorrhage of managerial talent to provider units, purchasers now find themselves caught in a trap at the same time as facing uncertainties created by major structural realignment.

But the suspicion must be that this will be a case of the hare and the tortoise. Henry Mintzberg was once noted as observing that the NHS was more of a policy than an organisation. The creation of trusts enhances the truth of that observation, with the focus of policy now becoming the purchasing authority. At the same time, the Health of the Nation (DH, 1991) seems to suggest that the policy will be increasingly about health gain rather than treatment of illness. In time, purchasers may find that the most appropriate method of delivering health gain is only partially through investment in illness treatment. Managers in provider units may in those circumstances find that they have gained an increased share of a cake that is diminishing. The activities of the provider managers explicitly to protect providers (and careers) as the impact of the Tomlinson

Report (1992) moves money from secondary treatment to primary care in London may well turn out to be the harbinger of a long-term trend. Cliff Graham's argument is that the NHS has been making steady progress towards an agenda focused on health over the past forty years and that the attention focused on trusts as a structural innovation may turn out to be as short lived as it is historically dubious.

However, there are likely to be gainers in that process as well as losers. Both of the provider chief executives featured in this book seem as confident of the potential long-term benefits to their organisations as they are enthusiastic about the short-term gain. But it is this focus on the needs of the individual organisation, rather than those of the broader NHS that is a major concern prompting the caution expressed by Andrew Wall.

Wall also raises doubts about the degree of accountability that boards represent. The weight of the arguments presented here is that boards have represented a major investment of management time as well as financial resources for, to date, a very limited return – very much as the researchers on commercial boards might have predicted. In addition, Trust Boards face two particular obstacles not normally confronted by their commercial counterparts. Firstly, the NHSME set out to try and recruit business people as non-executive directors who did not have product knowledge. Secondly, the NHS has a long tradition of health authority members and senior officers skilled in managing external input.

Finally, it is worth reflecting that contrary to the beliefs of some, trusts may not be the final chapter in the story of management restructing in the NHS. They may currently represent the NHS interpretation of wider managerial fashion. It is unlikely, given the accelerating pace of social and organisational change, that they will achieve a longevity of the teaching hospital board of governors upon which they are modelled. Recent overtures to the private sector to pursue joint ventures suggest that yet further new structures will evolve.

References

Department of Health (1989) 'Working for-Patients', Cmnd 555, London: HMSO.

Department of Health (1991) 'Health of the Nation', Cmnd 1523, London: HMSO.

Griffiths, R. (1983) NHS Management Inquiry. London: Department of Health and Social Security

Harrison, S., Hunter D., Marnoch, G. and Politt, C. (1992) Just Managing: Power and Culture in the National Health Service, London: MacMillan.

Health Committee (1992) *NHS Trusts: Interim Conclusion and Proposals for Future Inquiries* London: HMSO.

Mark, A. and Scott H. (1992) 'Management of the National Health Service' in Willcocks I. and Harrow J. *Rediscovering Public Service Management* London: McGraw-Hill.

National Health Services Management Inquiry, (1983), (1st Griffiths Report), London, Department of Health and Social Security.

Report of the Inquiry into London's Health Service, Medical Education and Records (1992), (Tomlinson Report), London: HMSO.